# The Drift

# The Drift

## STOPPING AMERICA'S SLIDE TO SOCIALISM

# Kevin A. Hassett

**FORMER CHAIRMAN OF THE PRESIDENT'S COUNCIL
OF ECONOMIC ADVISERS**

Regnery
1947 | **75**YEARS | 2022
WASHINGTON, D.C.

Regnery® is a registered trademark and its colophon is a trademark of Salem Communications Holding Corporation

ISBN: 978-1-68451-265-2
eISBN: 978-1-68451-266-9

Published in the United States by
Regnery Publishing
A Division of Salem Media Group
Washington, D.C.
www.Regnery.com

Manufactured in the United States of America

10 9 8 7 6 5 4 3 2 1

Books are available in quantity for promotional or premium use. For information on discounts and terms, please visit our website: www.Regnery.com.

*To Kristie Stokes Hassett*

# CONTENTS

# Preface

***Merriam-Webster Dictionary:***

*Drift*: "[S]omething driven, propelled, or urged along or drawn together in a clump . . ."

## Hassett's Dictionary:

*The Drift*: "The tendency of a capitalist society that has long prospered with free speech and free markets to produce intellectuals, politicians, institutions and media that propel said society toward socialism and totalitarianism."

## CHAPTER ONE

# The Trump Legacy: Disrupting the Drift toward Socialism

**M**ost Americans are still gobsmacked by the tumultuous and surreal four years of the Trump administration. What did we just go through? It's a question on everyone's mind, but answers are hard to come by.

Assessing any presidency is difficult, but giving an account of the Trump presidency has been complicated by the desire of most of the American media to destroy the man. On just about every issue, the media have done everything in their power to make Donald Trump look bad. The most egregious examples, such as the Russia hoax or their coverage of the coronavirus's originating in a Wuhan laboratory, involved downright fabrications—several steps beyond the liberal bias Americans have come to expect from the mainstream press.

Americans have known that the press look for negative stories, but this time was different. Anything that might hurt Trump—no matter how poorly sourced or salacious—was considered fair play, while worthy areas of inquiry that might help him politically were set out of bounds, such as the question of what Hunter Biden was up to in China or Ukraine.

When it comes to anything related to Donald Trump, neutral observers can no longer trust most sources about most topics.

During the Trump presidency, that mentality fanned out beyond President Trump himself. Now, the press are completely in the tank for the Democrats in a way that few could have predicted a decade or so ago. Journalists inflect coverage of most events with their political biases. They consider it a moral obligation to contort public opinion to the benefit of their favorite politicians.

But why do some politicians become the chosen ones? And why do others get cancelled, removed from polite society, and de-platformed? How does Donald Trump fit into the arc of history that has brought us to this crazy time?

This book answers those questions. And the first part of the story requires an honest and factual look at the presidency of Donald Trump. A fair-minded student of history believes not just what she reads in the press, but also the historical accounts of those who were close to a president. The idea that Donald Trump was not treated fairly requires knowledge of what an honest account might have looked like if the man were truly visible to the outside world.

Some presidents are builders, some are managers, and some are wartime leaders. And a few, like Donald Trump, are disruptors and transformers who redefine their times. The main thesis of this book is that Donald Trump was not a crazy outlier but a logical response to the forces that had taken over this country when he came into office. Trump disrupted and transformed a country that was drifting inexorably towards socialism, which anyone who believes in the idea of America should despise. Fighting against that Drift requires understanding Donald Trump and the forces he was fighting against. Crowds at Trump rallies exhibited a euphoria analogous to early Beatles concerts, and they did so not so much because they loved the man, but because they loved a man who was willing to fight to preserve the country they love.

From my time as one of the president's closest advisers, I have a unique perspective on both the man and the mass of agendas arrayed against him. Across the four years of the Trump presidency, I had a close working relationship with this presidential agent of change. I watched him forcefully challenge Washington's mire of special interests and corrupt politics which was first labelled "the swamp" by Ronald Reagan. I saw first-hand how discerning Donald Trump was in private discussions while publicly he projected a personal style of audacity that forced a degree of balance on a relentlessly biased media and hostile status quo. I helped him devise and enact economic policies that left no doubt that free market policies work, yielding jobs and better incomes for the American people, especially those at the bottom.

For more than two of those years, I served the president as chairman of the Council of Economic Advisers (CEA). I helped President Trump shape trade policies that put American workers before foreign interests. I worked with him and his top advisors to craft tax cuts that resulted in long-overdue wage increases for Americans.

After our success in passing tax cuts that revived the economy, I was brought into the Oval Office to offer guidance in other policy arenas. During the COVID crisis, I was brought back as senior advisor to the president to help devise the economic response to the pandemic recession. (I like to joke that I am the only person who has ever been both an Adviser and an advisor to the president.)

The president had me on speed dial because he understood that hard data and economics define what is possible in public policy—whether reversing weak economic growth, putting together a peace proposal for the Middle East based on rising living standards, or countering the bitter pain of pandemic shutdowns.

It wasn't clear then—but as the Biden years begin, it is clear to many of us now—that Donald Trump, for all his flaws, represented what might have been the last stand of the America we know against a strong current toward socialism and "woke" tyranny. By 2019, millennials were telling pollsters they would vote for a socialist candidate.[1] Once-moderate Democrats and even a fair number of ostensibly conservative Republicans are caught in the socialist Drift. They advocate a degree of government regulation of business that would spell the end of this country's heritage of free markets and personal liberty.

But Trump's battle need not be the last stand. Understanding the stakes of this fight should lead everyone, Democrat and Republican alike, to stand up and renew the battle before it is too late. We have too much to lose to remain divided by petty feuds. The Drift towards socialism is real. Donald Trump saw that and fought against it. We need to do the same or risk losing the things we hold dear.

★ ★ ★

My time running the Council of Economic Advisers in Donald Trump's White House was intense. I have never worked harder or had more fun in a job. And it almost cost me my life.

With my team of economists, experts, and writers at CEA, our office often felt more like the newsroom of a daily newspaper in the days before the internet than a quiet think tank. We were always writing, talking, debating, collaborating, and editing. I asked my staff to do a back-of-the-envelope check on how much material we churned out. I was astonished to find that we poured an estimated 4 million words into public documents and confidential White House memos during my time at CEA.

I had a rule that nothing went out before I had a chance to look at it. That meant I stayed in the office long after everybody else went home. I would attend heated White House meetings all day, and then around 6:00 p.m. I would begin poring over all of the documents that my staff had produced that day. I would go home around 9:00 p.m., see my family, and have a late dinner. Then the next day, I'd be back to the White House, often very early in the morning.

An unofficial part of my job was explaining administration policies and economic outcomes to the media. At the encouragement of President Trump and White House Press Secretary Sarah Sanders, I went on television to discuss economics many times a week. I was perhaps the only member of the Trump White House who was a regular not just on Fox, but also on CNN and MSNBC. I formed close friendships with journalists, such as Ali Velshi at MSNBC, who spent most of their time in an all-out war with the White House. A friend once joked that my biggest flaw is that I see the good in everybody rather than the truth. That weakness, perhaps, made it possible for me to work with the hostile media.

I've worked at such a pace all my life, and I've always found recovery from hard work in little oases during the day—breaks for a workout, my classical guitar, or an aikidō class, time with the family at dinner and on the weekends. Despite working close to ninety hours a week, I had support from my wife and family. And I had the consolation of those physical outlets in the gym and on the mat to balance me out. But well into my job at CEA I began to feel a deep exhaustion that was unlike ordinary tiredness. One day in early 2018, I was about to go on MSNBC, all wired up facing the harsh lights, when I started to feel listless, like a deflating balloon.

It was a Friday afternoon and I was on "Pebble Beach"—that strip of concrete in front of the White House on which sits a little village of tents, providing the backdrop for network correspondents to do their television reports. I was waiting to do a "hit" (as everyone has come to call an interview. Given the bias in many of the interviews, it often felt like the journalists' idea of the meaning of "hit" was close to that of Tony Soprano) on MSNBC when my listlessness turned into a dizziness so severe that I thought I'd fall over. With the interview just a few seconds away, I began to struggle to catch my breath. I pulled the microphone off my shirt and pulled out my earpiece. I turned to the technician and said, "I must be having a blood sugar problem or something," I said. "I'm sorry, I can't do the hit." Maybe it was just fatigue. It was freezing outside. I had just done a number of interviews, and I had an old-fashioned New Englander's practice of not wearing a winter coat during hits, even when the temperatures were in the 20s.

My assistant, who always attended interviews with me, walked with me as I wobbled back to my car, parked as usual in a choice spot in the

West Executive parking lot next to the White House. Instead of calling an ambulance, I foolishly climbed in to drive to my doctor's office. I thought sitting behind the wheel might ease the dizzy spell. Instead, I started feeling intense pressure in my chest and like my heart was beating way too fast. I was dizzy again. But I didn't want to call 911. If an ambulance were called, my personal health crisis would be all over the news. I had visions of myself on the nightly news being taken out of the White House on a stretcher and all of my friends and family first finding out I was ill on television.

Better to sneak away to get medical help, I thought. It was a stupid decision that I was lucky to survive.

Once at my doctor's office, he gave me an electrocardiogram and found that my heart was beating at more than 170 beats per minute. A few minutes later, as I was being admitted to the hospital, a morbidly amusing question occurred to me: When the *Washington Post* ran the story about the demise of the chairman of the CEA, would I make the front page? Or would my story be above the fold on page two? Alongside the comics? I congratulated myself that at least I had made it to Sibley Hospital in D.C. without anyone knowing. Then, even in my pain, I had to laugh at myself for worrying about such vanities.

As bad as my heart problem seemed at the time, it was in fact worse. After spending a night at one hospital, I was put in a special cardiac ambulance and taken to another with more advanced cardiac facilities. When they went inside and looked, they found much to fix. Two operations and ten days later I came out with a repaired heart that was, for the most part, back to normal.

My wife, Kristie, and I resolved to tell no one the extent of my heart procedures, not my staff, not even John Kelly, Donald Trump's second White House chief of staff. Gary Cohn, the chair of the National Economic Council, is the only person I informed, but I did tell him that he could share it with anyone he felt he needed to. I didn't want people to be concerned that when I recovered I wouldn't be ready to come back and tackle the job. And I did not want to excite rumors among those

White House staffers who had wanted me out of the Trump White House from the beginning. Any White House is a pool of sharks, and a little bit of blood in the water will turn you into a snack. One late Thursday I had my final procedure, spent a couple of days recovering in the hospital, then went back to work on a Monday, expecting a quiet day catching up, letting everyone know I had recovered from "the flu."

Hoping to ease my way into the slipstream, however, turned out to be about as realistic as easing into the Daytona 500.

Shortly after my return, the president called me to the Oval Office to go over the latest economic news. He liked the positive data on employment and growth so much that he asked me to handle the day's White House press conference and announce the good news. "Yes, sir!" I responded. It was perhaps not as foolish as my drive to the hospital in the first place. Modern medicine is a wonderful thing.

I went back to the White House because I felt a calling to serve my country, full stop. I chose to write this book because amidst all the emotion and anger surrounding the Trump administration, someone without a hidden agenda needed to step up and describe what happened and what it was like to work in that White House. Somebody who was trusted and respected by the president and his team but could also go on MSNBC and have a calm and productive conversation with opposition pundits. I wanted to write that book, one that I believe people will want—even need—to read. This is a book about the Trump years, what they tell us about where we are today, and what the choices ahead are for America as we drift headlong into socialism.

★ ★ ★

My first six months in the White House were consistent with the idea most people have of the early days of the Trump presidency. It was chaos.

President Trump had built a team of rivals in his White House. As tough as the fire was from outside, the fire from inside ran even hotter. It is said that the Inuit people have fifty words for snow, ranging from "qanuk" which means snowflake, to "nutaryuk" which means fresh snow.[2] In the Trump White House, we joked that we needed fifty words for different kinds of stress. The cumulative strain took a physical toll on all of us. About a year later, incoming National Economic Council chair Larry Kudlow had a very similar health experience to my own, suffering the most severe physical consequences from the constant pressure.

There were lots of reasons for me to stay away from the Trump White House, not least of which was the promise of constant rivalry and stress. Before I even met him, the forty-fifth president's blunt take on my profession was just as foreboding. As a bottom-line guy, Trump hated the equivocations and hedged predictions of economists. (Economists are so apt to say, "on the other hand," that President Harry Truman once exclaimed: "Give me a one-handed economist!"[3]) Donald Trump was so distrustful of the profession that he had evicted the CEA from the Cabinet. There was even a rumor that the president did not even want to appoint a CEA chair until he was told that the appointment was required by statute.

I also knew that if I said "yes" to this administration, I would be saddled with plenty of President Trump's baggage. His enemies absolutely despised him, and even a trip outside to talk about the latest jobs numbers or some other boring economic fact would elicit ridicule and even death threats. The barrage from the media, the opposition, and many in the public was nasty, meanspirited, and often idiotic. It has been a tradition for chairmen of the Council of Economic Advisers to be deferential to their successors out of respect for how difficult the job can be. Such courtesy was not afforded the Trump economic team, with senior Obama administration officials swinging for the fences with nasty ad hominem attacks on Twitter and television virtually every day. Clearly, a large swath of polite society wanted every Trump appointee to know that the decision to work for the man was a career-ending one.

But the arguments for going in outweighed these considerations. The Trump administration had offered senior positions to only a few professional economists. If I didn't take it, who would? I believed from the get-go that Donald Trump had great instincts. I believed that America had reached an inflection point, at which we would either restore vigor to the capitalist system as a means of human improvement and social advancement or become a socialist country. If we chose the latter, the special character of our nation would be lost. We would no longer be exceptional in any meaningful way. In a very real sense, we'd no longer be America. And I could tell from his speeches and remarks that Donald Trump thought the same way I did.

As I said, the forty-fifth president had great instincts. But unless those instincts were informed by professional advice, the result would be failure. So with a mixture of curiosity and a desire to serve, I took the offer to head CEA.

I have never regretted that decision, even if it did eventually contribute to heart problems. I set off on a journey that tested my beliefs, rounded out my perspective, and forced me to prioritize certain ideals. It was a journey of discovery, both for myself and my fellow Americans.

* * *

President Trump is gone now, but the stresses and fracture lines revealed by that conflict are still with us. What's more, the victors control the spoils, and a concerted effort is clearly underway to erase President Trump from history. His Twitter account is gone. Conservatives who defend him are liable to be erased from Amazon and exiled from Twitter and Facebook. The television media, outside of Fox News, has apparently forgotten he ever existed. His critics clearly hope that what is left of his legacy will be visions of insurrection, a Capitol under siege, and a president who was resoundingly condemned by his own majority leader.

Love Donald Trump or hate him, that cannot be allowed to happen. Far from erasing Trump from history, we must define Donald Trump's place in history if we are to understand our times and the challenges ahead. A dispassionate and careful record of the Trump presidency will be necessary to help us get back on track as a country. Was he as crazy in person as MSNBC anchors asserted? How did Donald Trump's Oval

Office meetings function? What were the beliefs behind his economic and foreign policy? How did his policies work? He claimed he wanted to help middle- and low-income Americans who had been poorly served by the wealthy elite. Did he accomplish that? Was his political demise (or at least setback if he decides to run again) the revenge of the elite, or the failure of his policies?

The first step to understanding Trump as a phenomenon is to take a deeper look at the workings of his White House and to follow the development and impact of his policies. As we will see, Donald Trump was, for the economic team at least, a surprisingly kind and effective leader in private, with a firm grasp on economic policy and a broad view of the historic conflict he was engaged in. You can't really understand Donald Trump without also understanding his own grasp of his place in history.

Donald Trump will be one of the most written-about American presidents for decades, if not centuries. The conflict between Trump and the Left will prove just as important historically. In pivotal moments, political tensions always risk boiling over. Trump's confrontation with the Left was as bitter as the partisan feuding in the election of 1800 between John Adams and Thomas Jefferson, an election that had tremendous consequences for the direction of the nascent American Republic. It is reminiscent of Andrew Jackson's fight with John Quincy Adams. Indeed, America is undergoing a crisis of legitimacy unlike any since the Civil War. Now as then, there is a sense that the existing constitutional order is collapsing and something new is taking shape.

But why? And why now?

* * *

When I was a kid in the 1960s, most people received their television over the airwaves, with antennae on roofs and blizzardy signals. Back then, a person's window to the outside world was a black-and-white television screen with news content that was arranged each day like a fresh diorama at the Museum of Natural History in New York. The curators of those windows were the news teams at the major networks. Walter Cronkite and then Dan Rather made sense of it all for us. Even through difficult times like the Vietnam War and the murder of Martin Luther King Jr., they were able to calmly and gracefully present the news.

In those days, the curators of the networks had the heavy responsibility of deciding which events rose to the level of importance that they should be presented to us in the limited time they had available. If you didn't like a news broadcast, your only choice then was to switch back and forth between the very similar perspectives of the three network news shows. These days, there are many choices, and a raging competition for our attention is under way. Even investigative journalists for the handful of prestigious national, digital newspapers must frame their stories as morality narratives, chock full of heroes, victims, and villains to get as many "clicks" as possible. The internet incentivizes outrage, and thus the most outrageous people always seem to win this competition for attention and harshness, while the rest of us wish this new harshness would go away.

Almost every American has a vague sense that our country is hurtling in the wrong direction. Angry people online have abandoned all pretense of grace or courtesy. The nastiness between people on the right and the left has risen to the point where Americans are literally shooting at one another. Moderate Republicans and Democrats might wish for a day where sensible, reasonable people represent their parties, but hard-line socialists and outrageously offensive conservative tweeters dominate the discussion.

Trump's superpower was that he understood this new reality and embraced it with gusto. While he was outrageous enough to addict social media users to his every word, he governed in a sensible and effective way. Left-wing attention getters such as Congresswoman Alexandria Ocasio-Cortez can shock with provocative statements. Her real shockers, however, are her radical, socialist policy prescriptions, including a

"Green New Deal" that would subject the entire economy to Soviet-like central control.

The frenzied national political dialogue has weakened the center and has destabilized society. We are wobbling on an unsteady axis. Society is getting coarser, and the revolution in how we communicate in a digital age is a leading cause.

In a sense this coarseness was one of several factors that led to the Trump presidency. But this era, for all its pitfalls and ugliness, may yet reverse the nation's Drift into socialism. Self-described socialist Bernie Sanders had enormous political success calling on Americans to abandon capitalism, a radical thought that attracted maximum attention. President Trump was a bulwark against that agenda—an agenda tacitly shared by large parts of the Democrat establishment, as we now see as "moderate" Joe Biden pursues a radical agenda. And though it might seem like Democrats hate Trump for his personality, their ire towards him comes from his effective unmasking of their aims. The Left hates Trump because he was an effective opponent of their socialist revolution.

The Left's radical shift represents a sea change in American politics. When President Obama took his historic place in the White House in 2008, his victory was so complete that he controlled the House of Representatives and the Senate, the latter with a supermajority. He and his party could enact whatever laws they wanted. They did not turn America into a socialist country, but they contributed to the slow leftward Drift.

But today, it is not just Bernie Sanders promoting socialism. It's almost the entire radicalized Democratic Party. In July 2020, Democratic presidential nominee Joe Biden said that capitalism is a "farce," and that "it's way past time to put an end to shareholder capitalism."[4] We live in a time when the rule of law upon which a free society is based is optional in major cities from New York to Chicago, Portland, and Seattle. This is a time when Antifa engages in the same intellectual sleight-of-hand socialists in England practiced during the Second World War, redefining anti-fascism as anti-capitalism while extolling the promised wonders of Marxism (without, of course, ever invoking the name of their prophet).

This is a time when the police that enforce the rule of law are threatened with slashed budgets and assaulted without penalty.

Why are we suddenly so close to the socialist edge? The renowned economist Joseph Schumpeter saw our age coming from almost a century ago. He wrote that socialists would take over our institutions of higher learning, indoctrinate our children to despise capitalism, gradually take control of the media, and make it so disreputable to defend capitalism that respectable people would shrink from the task. The details of his analysis, which we will dig into in the last third of the book, are so precisely descriptive of today, that one wonders whether he possessed a time machine. Socialism would win, he wrote, because there would be no one left to defend the free market.[5] The current exaltation of socialists by the traditional media and the academic community was the precise culmination of the process Schumpeter foresaw almost one hundred years ago.

But there is hope, and it stems from the competition for attention that produced both Bernie Sanders and Donald Trump. We now live in the internet age, the "media" that were so important to Schumpeter's theory are radically different now. A description of the likely evolution of society must factor in how people communicate and disseminate information. We see in the People's Republic of China that the power of social media and machine intelligence give Big Brother far more power to observe and oppress than in the past. But the information pipeline also flows both ways. While the Left's captive media bombard Americans with propaganda, citizens are taking to social media to effectively correct, counter, and balance the media's narratives. Nowhere is that clearer than in the success of truth-tellers in exposing Anthony Fauci's apparent prevarications regarding the origin of the Wuhan virus, whose lethal gain-of-function experiments may have been funded with American taxpayer dollars directed by Fauci himself.[6] The idea was banned from social media and taboo in the mainstream media. But because the theory was more plausible than the alternatives, a thousand tiny voices kept it alive.

Oxford University's Chris Kutarna also saw Trump coming before almost anyone else and defined his emergence better than anyone else:

I don't think that we've *begun* to realize the power that social media has given to everyone. I only have to look at President Donald Trump, at the stranglehold that he has on our attention, to see that we don't yet understand our full power. Again, this is something that Marshall McLuhan made clear fifty years ago. He said that when we enter into the digital age, we're going to *regress* to an oral culture. We're going to regress to a society in which *who* says a thing and *how big* an audience hears the saying of it determines what's true for us. . . . We still have a long way to go toward recognizing our power to ignore—and on the flipside, how *we* are the oxygen feeding the bonfires we can't look away from.[7]

Social media has fundamentally altered the socialist calculus. On the one hand, the ability of a centralized authority to control citizens is greatly advanced by the privacy-destroying tools available to governments. On the other hand, as nasty as social media can be, the monolithic media that ensured victory for Hillary Clinton and the Left were knocked over by Donald Trump, who was always one step ahead in the competition for attention that social media creates. His outrageousness was a precondition for his victory.

Donald Trump tweeted his way past the media that had been captured by the Left, and appealed directly to voters. He was a marketing genius who forced the media that were hostile but hungry for ratings to cover his rallies and provide him with a free presidential ad campaign. He was willing to take the heat from the intellectual elite that energetically ridiculed everything from his capitalist convictions to his hair. And for four years, he triumphed. The gatekeepers could not contain him. The real battle all along was Trump versus socialism, and for a while, Trump won.

In the chapters to come, I'll tell you a very personal story of how I saw the president stand up to socialism and reverse a stagnant economy and the rising inequality of the Obama years. We will look carefully at how the socialist elite struck back, explain why society has become so crazy, and determine what we can do—with or without Donald Trump—to preserve our country.

## CHAPTER TWO

# Trial by Trump

"**Y**ou're a handsome guy," Donald Trump said to me as I walked in for my first Oval Office meeting in late spring 2017. I was there to brief the president on the economic condition of the country six months after President Obama had left office. His greeting filled me with trepidation about his eyesight.

"Thank you, sir," I said, quite obviously a little flustered. "I actually don't get that very often," I added.

The president sat behind the Resolute desk, carved from the timbers of the HMS *Resolute* as a gift from Queen Victoria to President Rutherford B. Hayes in 1880. Donald Trump gave me an appraising glance as he sipped his ever-present Diet Coke. Over the course of that first meeting and every subsequent one, a White House butler would appear every fifteen minutes to quietly replace the president's Diet Coke so the ice would never melt. The top of the desk had an ominous box near the president with a single button in the middle. I first thought it was "the button." But thirty seconds after he pushed it, a Diet Coke arrived rather than nuclear attack. That moment between the push and the arrival of the Coke remains one of the longest in my life.

I proceeded to march through a printout of a number of charts, sitting next to his desk, flipping through from slide to slide. The headline was that the nation in early 2017 was still in the grip of President Obama's policies, promoting a very uneven recovery. The charts showed some states were red-hot, where jobs were plentiful and houses for sale flew off the market. Other states were still sluggish and falling behind.

Florida was one of the sluggish ones, I told the president. Housing prices were falling. He bolted forward.

"That's not right," the president said. "Kevin, I know Florida, and there's no way that's true. No way."

If I had been wrong about that, of course, I had no business briefing the president on anything. I assured him the data were correct, that housing prices in Florida were dropping. He assured me they were not. I realized the next few seconds would determine whether I could work for the forty-fifth president.

"Sir," I said, "these numbers are absolutely correct. I will never present you with any fact that hasn't been thoroughly vetted and verified."

I went on to explain to the president that the Florida market that he knew—the multimillion-dollar estates along the coast, especially those of the Palm Beach neighbors of his beloved Mar-a-Lago resort—were doing just fine. The condos, townhouses, and modest homes further inland were not, especially in the panhandle.

The president relaxed and smiled. He seemed satisfied.

I later learned that this was not an incidental blowup. Donald Trump usually challenged new people, in one instance telling a briefer, "that was a piece a shit." Those who fumbled, apologized, or folded had a short tenure in the White House. Those who pushed back won the president's trust. And yes, swearing was common.

I had won the president's trust. But could I keep it?

I was nominated but far from being confirmed as the president's chief economist as chairman of the Council of Economic Advisers. Steve Bannon—caricatured by the White House press corps as the president's grizzled, unkept Svengali—was at that time a near constant presence hovering around the Oval Office, meeting often with the president, but never in my memory at meetings with other senior White House staff. Steve is a bright and engaging man. He and I hit it off right away when exchanging ideas in the hallways of the West Wing and in his office across the way from Chief of Staff Reince Priebus. But I knew that despite our friendly interactions, Steve was likely behind frequent attacks on me at Breitbart News, labeling me as a "globalist" who needed to be nixed before I could undermine the Trump agenda. Breitbart News reported: "If Hassett is confirmed, that will be a win for the corporatist, business-first faction in Trump's White House, which fights for influence in the Oval Office against the populist, America-first faction that helped Trump win the election."[1]

As spring gave way to summer in 2017, my being confirmed to the post grew more and more unlikely. Not only had I somehow become a bête noire of the populist right, I was also facing growing skepticism about my nomination from prominent U.S. senators from both parties.

I was getting it from the left and the right.

Throughout the summer, I continued to enjoy my interactions with the president. His free-flowing give and take was a refreshing change from the anxious conversations that so often define Washington. Though I had a background as a conventional Republican economist and proponent of international trade, I was genuinely sold on Trump's agenda. Liberating capitalism from the shackles of Obama-era regulations to lift Americans back to prosperity, making the tax code more friendly for businesses that create jobs, and bringing balance back to trade agreements were all essential to creating a robust economy. I was eager to help the president implement that agenda.

I signed up with Donald Trump knowing that some in my own party might never forgive me. Like many, I was wary of his public persona, of the guy who was much ruder than any politician in my memory. But I did so because Trump saw truths in plain sight ignored by political professionals and coastal elites. Trump had an exquisite understanding of working Americans because he listened to them. My academic work showed that policies like Trump's were exactly what blue collar workers needed to see their lives improve. He was passionate about making their lives better, and so was I.

He saw the distance between public-sector unions (pro-tax, anti-industry) and private-sector unions (pro-pipelines and skeptical of big government and taxes). He realized the opportunity to transform the Republican Party from a movement driven by rich donors into a home for working men and women.

He saw in the widening disparity between Democratic rhetoric and its shameful performance for minority communities a chance to win the hearts, minds, and votes of black and Latino voters.

He saw that all Americans—Latinos included—are appalled and frightened by a government that doesn't take its borders or citizenship seriously. Donald Trump saw the carnage left behind as America drifted into socialism.

He also had a winning way of bringing his skill in marketing to politics. Think about it: Donald Trump used rallies and Twitter to force a hostile media and social-media companies to serve as his personal ad agencies. Love him or hate him, there was a genius to that. Jared Kushner, who had watched Trump up close for years as his son-in-law, told me a story that highlighted how clever Trump was. During the Republican primaries, Jared recalled, President Trump drove the conversation but spent almost no money. All of his press was free. But as the general election approached, the campaign recognized that they would have to ramp up the organization and spend more money. So they started marketing MAGA hats. Jared recalled that their profits from hat sales alone were enough to fund a good chunk of the general election campaign.

Donald Trump understood how to use audacity to drive attention, and how to use anger and overstatement to convince voters that unlike other politicians, he really meant it. He was the disruptor we needed.

I was sold on the topline Trump agenda. In my time at the White House, I was thrilled with my good working relationship with the president, even if I was at times turned off by his ugly side frequently expressed on Twitter.

As the months dragged in the spring and summer of 2020, the attacks on me escalated, and the Senate dragged its feet on my nomination. It seemed like it wouldn't be long before I was ushered to the door.

★ ★ ★

Breitbart was right about one thing. I didn't have the DNA of a Trump advisor.

I had taught at the Columbia Business School and held an endowed chair at the American Enterprise Institute (AEI). I wasn't on board with Trump when we all watched him take the golden escalator down to announce his candidacy. Even worse in the eyes of Breitbart, I had been an economic advisor to the presidential campaigns of George W. Bush, John McCain, and Mitt Romney. Little wonder that I was seen by many as another establishment anti-Trump Republican with all the markings of a muck-dwelling swamp creature.

John McCain and I had been particularly close. I worked with John to build his economic team for his first presidential campaign back in 2000. I often rode on his Straight Talk Express, where it was hard to get any work done because the senator was such a continuous cut-up. When I was nominated for CEA, John McCain gave an endorsement of me on the Senate floor, where he said with customary McCain humor that the only time he had ever doubted my intelligence was when I agreed to work for him.

I also saw John McCain's principled side. During the Arizona senator's first presidential campaign in 2000, social conservative Gary Bauer launched an ugly attack on McCain for proposing to allow gays to serve in the military. Bauer whipped up a furor among some evangelicals. Getting on an elevator with the senator and his wife, Cindy, McCain said to me, "I can't believe I'm in a party that's filled with such bigotry."

For all of the Washington rumors about his thin skin, the only time I ever saw him get angry was on behalf of other people.

I was an economic advisor in four Republican campaigns, but after Romney lost in 2016, I invested my energy in launching a project with Matt Jensen, a colleague at AEI, to potentially get involved in all campaigns. One thing I learned about campaigns is that they are supposed to be about policy, but the complicated apparatus needed to conduct analysis is too costly for any campaign to build out. Candidates want to have proposals that make the country a better place and present results that describe what they cost and how they will work. But only the big government bureaucracies like the Congressional Budget Office (CBO) have the tools needed to assess policy proposals. In my view, that hamstrings political debate and policy innovation, so I decided to retire from politics and build a virtual CBO that could help candidates of any party design and score whatever policy their heart desired. The hope was that the competition of ideas that ensued would make our country better.

Matt and I created the Open Source Policy Center, an interactive website (OSPC.org) loaded with tools to help candidates form their platforms and conduct economic analysis. The tools are available to everyone of course, so you, dear reader, can develop your own plan right now if you would like to pause reading for a bit. It was a complex, expensive undertaking, though we got it done in record time. To this day, the Open Source Policy Center allows candidates to shape their policies and shows how those policies would affect jobs, growth, the federal budget, and other parts of the economy.

As Donald Trump began to solidify his hold on the Republican nomination, I started to read the work product of his campaign, economic papers that were appropriate as rhetorical statements for a primary, but that couldn't hold up to the scrutiny that a general election nominee would undergo. The campaign recognized this as well, and when a friend of Jared Kushner's contacted me with a request from the campaign for help, I was happy to pitch in, just as I had for other campaigns from both parties in that cycle. So I contacted the campaign and helped Trump's economic team plug their policies into our website. I also connected them with an economist who was adept at running our software, and they brought this fellow into the campaign. The result was a slew of papers that were better grounded, more credible, and, most important for Trump, the constant barrage of stories that "Trump's numbers don't add up" stopped. The campaign was grateful, and my help was noted.

It didn't hurt my relationship with the campaign that I had penned a piece in Bloomberg years before in which I said Donald Trump had the makings of a strong presidential candidate. Unlike most "establishment" Republicans, I took him as a serious candidate right from the start. It struck me even then that if he were ever to be elected president, he would recognize the Drift and confront it in a blunt and effective way. He had a reputation for being a problem-solver. And on *The Apprentice* he came across as tough but having good judgment. And in the end, he seemed to care about the people on the show, which made him appear a good guy. Real or not, those were great attributes for a candidate to display.[2]

Like millions of other Americans, I had a sense of Trump's impending victory as the 2016 campaign came to a close despite the lopsided polls and confident prognosticators indicating the contrary. Not long after Donald Trump's victory, I heard from an old friend and colleague, David Malpass, an international economist and now president of the World Bank, who asked if I would consider an appointment in the new administration.

I told David I was interested and that we should talk about it. I was soon summoned to the Trump Hotel in Washington, D.C., where I met with Steven Mnuchin, slated to become Treasury secretary, and some of the transition staff. Steven had come from the world of investment banking and hedge funds. Just after, I met with Gary Cohn at the Four Seasons Hotel in Georgetown. Gary had made a fortune in commodities trading and at Goldman Sachs. Both men were headed for the Cabinet, and I knew that they were looking for a compatible third-wheel in economic policy.

Gary and Steven were personal friends of one other but quite different fellows. Gary is an affable back-slapping bundle of charisma. Steven is a reserved, precise details guy. In those meetings, both were straight-shooters who were low-key but solid in their declarations. I had apparently done well in our interview. Gary asked me over for breakfast to hold a deeper discussion on the complexities of working in the Trump White House, gauging whether I was really up to the challenge. I had a short interview with President-elect Donald Trump, but he told Gary and Steven to pick the CEA chair they liked best.

Any president's economic team is governed by "the Troika"—the Treasury secretary, the director of the Office of Management and Budget, and the chair of the Council of Economic Advisers. Steven Mnuchin was to become Treasury Secretary. Congressman Mick Mulvaney was set to head OMB. And I was to chair the CEA.

Gary would run the National Economic Council (NEC), which coordinates economic policy across the government. So the Troika made policy, and Gary and the NEC made it happen. Together, the four of us worked quickly, informally, and decisively. We decided early on not to let bureaucracy get between us. We operated more like the partners of an opportunistic hedge fund than departmental and agency heads who communicated by staff or by memo.

As the head of the Council of Economic Advisers, I chaired the Troika, which meant I had the last word in making the economic and budgetary assumptions for the president's budget.

CEA was a product of the Truman administration, created in 1946 to help prevent future depressions. At the time, the government was still running an economy centralized for a war we had already won. Many leading politicians, including former Vice President Henry A. Wallace, had concluded that the success of wartime production validated the idea of making America into a socialist country. Truman, who replaced Wallace on FDR's ticket, may have been a liberal but he was no socialist. Truman fought communism abroad and worked hard to keep the left wing of his party from drifting in that direction. His advisors drew up a plan for the CEA to serve as a bulwark against socialism. The CEA created a structured way to bring in smart and talented economic minds to spell out facts that, if candidly presented, ought to naturally guide policy makers to support capitalism and the free market.

As President Trump planned how to reverse Obama's economic centralization and its impact on the economy, he found CEA a natural tool. It had a degree of independence set in stone, so our advice couldn't be distorted by other advisors within the White House or political fads rippling through the Trump movement. And it had clout. While many senior people in the White House have little to no staff, I had fifty people working for me. This gave the CEA chair the ability to produce quality economic data and insights on-demand on virtually any topic.

I was given the CEA job well before Trump's inauguration, but the path from there to officially having the job went through a field of land-mines. First, the Office of Government Ethics has to go over your finances and recommend changes to your holdings in order to make sure there are no conflicts with your work responsibilities. This was my first experi-ence with the deep state. While my finances were simple, the OGE slow-rolled my paperwork to such an extent that my attorney, who had worked in the Obama administration, called the head of the office to complain. Those liberal bureaucrats clearly wanted Trump appointees to drop out, frustrated by the process, or at the very least to carry on their duties hamstrung by restrictions placed on nominees yet to be confirmed. It was frustrating and got under my skin.

★ ★ ★

If you've ever wondered what it is like to sprint across a shooting range, try being a Trump nominee to a position that requires Senate confirmation. I had to testify before the Senate Banking, Housing, and Urban Affairs Committee. In the early stage of a nomination, it is cus-tomary for a nominee to make courtesy visits to each of the senators on the committee. One of the committee's more well-known members is the senior senator from my home state of Massachusetts, Elizabeth Warren.

I was told that Elizabeth Warren was notoriously hard on nominees, that the last Trump nominee she took a meeting with was asked only one question then rudely escorted out of the office, punctuated by a slammed door. I steeled myself and went in to see the senator late one afternoon in the spring of 2017 in the Hart Senate Office Building.

To my relief, the senator smiled when I was escorted by staff into her inner office.

"I know we're going to disagree about a lot," she said, "but I think we can have some really good give and take."

My shoulders came down a notch. "Senator, I'm looking forward to it."

We shook hands, and I took a moment to take in Elizabeth Warren's office, her books and memorabilia. A glance confirmed that she was as much of a New England Patriots fan as I am. She invited me to sit, and we bonded over our devotion to our beloved football team. Senator Warren was particularly amused when I told her I had co-authored an academic analysis that showed why the team's "Deflategate" scandal was bogus. At issue was whether the New England Patriots had deliberately deflated their footballs before a playoff game with the Indianapolis Colts. I had worked with an AEI colleague, Stan Veuger, to question the metrics and methodology of the NFL-commissioned report. For example, were the Colts' footballs measured earlier in the day, when it was colder?[3]

Such a nerdy approach to sports amused her as much as a spirited defense of our team.

With a friendly connection established, Senator Warren asked me a series of well-informed, substantive questions about the state of finance and the impact of regulation on the economy. We both relaxed and proceeded to have a deep conversation with strong but respectful give and take. I wasn't surprised when Senator Warren capped our talk by appealing to me to be the "voice of reason" in the Trump White House. I thanked her and politely demurred. By the time the senator looked at her watch, the shadows outside her office window were lengthening into night. Senator Warren gave me a friendly handshake, and I left thinking that perhaps I might just have won her vote. On the way out, I stuck a pin in the map of Massachusetts that she has in her waiting room to show where I came from. The pin went into my hometown of Greenfield, Massachusetts.

The other memorable meeting I had was with Senator Bob Corker of Tennessee. I once again had my expectations upended, but this time not in a good way. Senator Corker was upset, though not at me in particular or at the president. He was seething over criticism from the think tank where I was a senior fellow, the American Enterprise Institute, because a scholar there had harshly criticized a bipartisan compromise on federal financial regulation the senator had crafted with his Democratic colleagues.

Corker was proud of his bipartisan achievement and believed the conservative scholar at AEI failed to understand the hard work it took to build a consensus on Capitol Hill between members of Congress with differing temperaments and values.

As Bob Corker spoke to me, he put a bitter spin on some choice words, complaining about *ivory tower intellectuals* in the *think tanks* who wanted the *perfect* legislation to stand in the way of the best possible legislation. Senator Corker also asked me pointedly if I had any idea what life was like for most Americans.

I assured him I understood the need for compromise in Washington and that I had nothing to do with that particular scholar's criticism of his policy. As far as being an out-of-touch academic, I told Senator Corker that I had been raised in a distressed community in Western Massachusetts. My first job was flipping burgers. I spent a summer working outdoors at a pickle factory. I made extra money helping farmers in my hometown stack bales of hay. I grew up with a keen appreciation of the economic problems most Americans suffer from because my own family suffered from them. In my public service I was driven to reduce taxes and regulations so we could help Americans like the people I grew up with.

That seemed to help. But I still left Senator Corker's office shaken. It was clear to me that he was considering blackballing my nomination just to stick a finger in the eye of AEI.

★ ★ ★

During my breakfast conversation with Gary Cohn at the Four Seasons, I asked him, if I accepted, if he would make sure my nomination was included in the first bundle of people sent up for confirmation in February to Capitol Hill. The Senate is notorious for moving at a slug's pace on nominations in the best of times. Washington was rife with rumors that the Democrats, though in the minority, would manipulate rules to make President Trump's process exceptionally slow and painful.

"The first package is going to be the Treasury secretary, the secretary of State, people like that," Gary said. At first I thought he was letting me down gently. "Schumer has told me that if we put forward a reasonable guy—and you definitely qualify as a reasonable guy—they'll just push you right through with them."

But even after my paperwork cleared, confirmations were being stonewalled by the Democrats in the Senate.

As the months rolled by and my nomination sat out there, the attacks on me intensified, not just from Breitbart but from other Trump-friendly outlets. The attacks that concerned me most came from Lou Dobbs on Fox Business Network, which I knew the president would see. The theme was the same in every attack: I was a globalist who would warp the president's agenda. I would undermine the president on immigration. I would eviscerate any effort to protect working Americans from unfair trade deals.

In short, I was dripping wet from the swamp.

This steady stream of attacks was, I believed at the time, inspired by Bannon, and probably also by Peter Navarro, who headed the Office of Trade and Manufacturing Policy established by President Trump. Peter and I would later become very close friends and remain so to this day, but no one would describe him as lacking sharp elbows. You might even say he is all elbows.

After seeing this kind of chatter in the far-right media, the president summoned me to meet with him again about my nomination. I took this as an ominous sign, figuring I was a goner. I went through the Oval Office, into the small conference room that he uses as a kind of home theater. The president was sitting in his favorite seat in front of the television, with Sarah Sanders at the other end of the table. Sarah had just done one of her first press conferences and was, I assumed, there to help manage the fallout from my withdrawal.

But instead, President Trump simply said, "There are a lot of people in this place who don't want you to get this job. But don't worry, I've got your back." That was all he had to say, so I thanked him and left. My head was spinning a bit. Why would he tell me that? Was he trying to reassure me, or warn me about a hostile workplace? Was he hoping I'd quit without being pushed?

I pondered those questions as I walked up the stairs of the West Wing to check in with Gary Cohn. On the way I ran into Ivanka Trump. When she asked how I was doing so far, I asked her to interpret her father's statement. She replied, "My father never has a hidden agenda in that kind of meeting. If he told you he has your back, it means he has your back." The rest of my tenure would prove her right.

At the other end of Pennsylvania Avenue, however, Democrats were stretching out debate for each nominee. The minority engaged in an unprecedented use of rules to obstruct the president from staffing his administration. As Senator Mitch McConnell wrote in *Politico*, "it took six months of partisan delays—and several railroad accidents—before Democrats let the Senate confirm a federal railroad administrator, even though none of them actually voted against the nominee at the end."[4] Hamstringing any administration in this way is not good for the country, and I have encouraged Republicans to treat President Biden's nominees, for the good of the country, with more consideration.

Every so often, I would check in with Marc Short, director of leg-islative affairs (and later chief of staff to Vice President Mike Pence), where my name was on the priority list. Between my colleagues' proxy attacks on me in conservative media and Democratic obstructionism, it looked as if my role in the Trump administration would be measured in Scaramucci units (more on that later).

* * *

My nomination hearing was at the Senate Banking Committee on June 6, 2017, with Senator Mike Crapo of Idaho presiding as chairman. Like most nominees, I showed up with my family—my wife, Kristie, and two sons, John and James—dutifully sitting behind me for moral support and, I will admit, for optics. The theory given to me by my Republican handlers on the committee is that the more a nominee's kids remain in a given senator's line of sight, the likelier it is the senator will refrain from planting a battle axe in said nominee's skull.

As I prepared to speak, I tried to keep in mind lessons from my training in aikidō, a martial arts discipline I have pursued diligently for years. In the dōjō, one prevails not by brute force, but by channeling an opponent's *ki* or energy into a position of imbalance. It is a gentle form of combat, meant to enervate and dissuade an opponent, to prevent and to deflect. The goal is not to win, but to gently demonstrate the futility of combat.

As the form requires, I was given a few minutes to make an opening statement. I told the committee:

> I have almost always been a student of economics, even before
> I knew it. I was raised by two public school teachers in the
> beautiful town of Greenfield, Massachusetts. My mother was
> a kindergarten teacher in neighboring Turners Falls. My
> father taught English at Greenfield High School and still lives
> in Greenfield in the same house I was raised in.

As I was growing up, my town went through a very painful transition. For the longest time, Greenfield was a thriving mill town, with the world's largest tap and die operation that employed thousands of citizens. Neighboring Turners Falls was almost as prosperous, housing a massive paper mill along the banks of the Connecticut River. But as we got older, times were changing. Plants closed. Families started moving away. Graduates stopped coming home after college.

It seemed impossible to look around and not wonder why it was happening. When I started studying economics in college, and again in graduate school, I always came back to the example of how my town changed. Why did plants move away or close? Why did many of the good jobs disappear? And is there something that policymakers can do to restore prosperity?

Economic models suggested a simple answer. Workers can have high wages if they have high productivity, and high productivity is enabled by an ample supply of productive capital. But going from things that work in textbook models to actual policy recommendations is a difficult thing. The real world has many complications that are not included in models, and the data often surprise economists, especially those who have too much confidence in pure theory.

That observation led me, over the years, to focus on things that can be learned from the data. My dissertation focused in part on how wages have moved over the business cycle. What do the periods when workers prosper have in common? My early career was spent studying how firms' investment decisions respond to government policy, and how labor and capital interact. . . .

I believe it is essential to gather evidence, and not just rely on theories. . . . Economic analysis should be transparent and replicable. [I described the mission and results of the Open

Source Policy Center at the American Enterprise Institute, casting perhaps a wary glance at Senator Corker.]

Finally, while I respect the need for all types of research, even the very theoretical, my own focus has mostly been work that holds the promise of improving the lives of others, and that sheds light on the circumstances of those less fortunate, like those in my hometown who lost their jobs when the factory closed.

When I finished, the questioning began.

Senator Catherine Cortez Masto of Nevada brought up a 2013 article in which I argued for the doubling of immigration. New workers, I had asserted, would spur economic growth to "restore our old normal."

"Here we are in 2017 with the administration pursuing precisely the opposite policies," Senator Cortez Masto said. "In fact the president's policy of pursuing mass deportation is sparking panic fear in Latino communities and causing consumer spending to fall by double digits." How could I serve in such an administration?

It was, of course, an invitation to suicide. I was being given an opportunity to make nice with Senator Cortez Masto and denounce my president, which would end my tenure before it began, or offend her and risk not being confirmed.

I took a deep breath and replied that economists are good at mapping inputs and outputs, and if we input more labor we will output more economic growth. But I stressed that I am an economist, not a policy maker, and that there were larger issues to consider about border security that transcended my advice and responsibilities.

But I did add that immigrants are more than twice as likely to be entrepreneurs than native-born Americans. They succeeded not because they were smarter or better credentialed, but because their willingness to pull up their roots proved they had gumption. "My ancestors were Irish immigrants," I said. "They weren't allowed in this country because they had a computer degree."

Senator Cortez Masto next wanted to know why I said that the "Wall Street reform," meaning the 2010 Dodd–Frank law regulating finance passed in a panic by Congress in the wake of the 2008 financial crash, "was the worst piece of legislation I've seen in my entire lifetime." It was, she quoted me, "lame-brained, horrifying legislation." And I was also told that I had said that it needed "to be repealed as soon as possible."

After hearing my words recited, I stammered for a moment. I didn't remember writing that or saying that. (I later learned that I did say those words on a heated exchange on Bloomberg TV in 2011.) It was, to be fair, a very hot take. Dodd–Frank was, in my estimation, a mélange of regulations that the big banks and financial institutions could easily cope with but which were a burden on smaller competitors. I could read in the senator's demeanor that she was offended. If I came back at her with a frontal response, I would be the one on the mat.

I apologized for my intemperate language. This upset some Republican committee staffers who felt that an apologizing witness risks looking weak and inviting more attacks, but it felt right.

And I said, "I am not usually so strident."

When Senator Corker's time came up, he warmly recognized my family and then proceeded to vent again about the American Enterprise Institute and think tanks in general. He said that when our courtesy meeting was over, "my temperature was about to take my head off . . . so many *think tanks* here in our Washington community make *the perfect* the enemy of the good and really can be destructive, very destructive, as we discussed, as we try to move ahead and actually pass legislation that accommodates some commonality on both the Republican and Democratic side. And actually the *think tank* that you've been a part of has played a big role in trying to undermine actually bipartisan efforts we've put together here on this committee. You and I discussed that fully."

I nodded, yes, we had.

"I thought of a person coming into the White House that had been quote, in an *ivory tower*, if you will, sitting over at a think tank *writing perfect things in a perfect world*, I then began to question whether someone like you would even be good in this position."

But then having made his point, the senator turned gracious.

"As my temperature cooled down and I thought a little bit more about your past. . . . Obviously you're qualified for this job," he said.

I thanked Senator Corker for taking the time to talk it through with me in our first meeting.

"A hallmark of my career is I have never been that person who says the perfect is the only thing you should do, and if you don't do that you're someone who is a traitor to economics," I said. I stressed that the role of the CEA is to provide objective advice and expert analysis so decision makers can make the best decisions. I noted that scholars at AEI have very strong opinions, they don't take my advice, and "I can assure that is not the way I would behave if confirmed."

So far, I was deflecting well.

Senator Corker then turned to a bestselling book I had written in 1999, *Dow 36,000*. It has since become something that no critic of Kevin Hassett could possibly overlook. The Dow Jones average at the time of my hearing in 2017 was a bit above 21,000, well short of what I had predicted. (At the time I'm writing, however, it is above 35,000.)

"Sir, I think that one critic of mine looked at that book and called it a 'youthful indiscretion,' and I think that as youthful indiscretions go, it was not such a bad one," I said, eliciting a few chuckles from Senator Corker and others. "I think the motivation of the book then was to make sure people understood how to think about equities and how . . . if you can be a good long-term investor, to invest in equities because they are a good investment in the long run but not in the short run. And I think that looking back, folks that bought and held were glad they did."

Senator Corker turned to my deviation from the president in trade.

"You're a full-blown free-trader," he said, wondering how I could serve in a protectionist administration.

I acknowledged that I had a history as an unabashed free-trader, but that my role was to provide the president with the best economic information. I also was on board with the idea of vetting our trade relationships with the national interest in mind. After a brief discussion of carried interest in tax policy, Senator Corker smiled and said, "I look forward to serving with you."

When it was Senator Warren's turn, she turned from me to focus her ire on my fellow nominee Pam Patenaude, up for a senior position at the Department of Housing and Urban Development. This was the clearest indication yet that I could count on her vote.

Going through a confirmation process is nerve-wracking, but I accept it as necessary. Catherine Cortez Masto and Bob Corker were constitutional officers, I was not. They had every right to press me with hard questions. I am just glad I had learned the discipline of defusing tough questions when an artless answer could have turned into a roadblock to my nomination.

* * *

I had hoped to be rapidly confirmed now that my hearing was over. One morning soon afterwards, I ran into Marc Short, then the White House legislative director.

"Hey, Kevin, good news," Marc said. "You're in the package."

And I was indeed in the package of nominees, my name ready to be moved along with those of other nominees to the floor for unanimous consent. Then I wasn't. At four that afternoon, I was singled out, a senator struck my name from the list.

It was rumored to have been Elizabeth Warren. I was surprised, but not too much. Senator Warren, after all, was a liberal Democrat with presidential ambitions for the 2020 election. Still, I was disappointed. I thought we had connected in our meeting, and, I confess, to this day I enjoy discussing issues with her.

As my nomination lingered, Gary Cohn, true to his word, stepped in to help me. He backed the "hotlining" of my nomination, expediting people the White House needed most. The Senate decided to proceed on the basis of unanimous consent for hotlined nominees in one package. I finally came up in one such package on September 12, 2017, eight months into the administration.

I was confirmed 81–16. My impressions from my courtesy calls were wrong. Senator Corker voted for me. Senator Warren voted against me, declaring, "The last thing we need is another economic adviser who wants to tilt the playing field even further in favor of corporate America."[5]

Oh well, at least Elizabeth and I will always have the Patriots!

Mike Pence swore me in in the vice president's Ceremonial Office, a Victorian rectangle with fireplaces of black marble; floors inlaid with mahogany, white maple, and cherry; and ornamental stencils on the ceilings and walls. Naval iconography was displayed throughout the room. Pence had given a gracious, informal speech saying that he had been a fan of Kevin Hassett "before it was cool." I thanked him afterwards and said, "Mr. Vice President, it's never been cool."

With Kristie, my sons, and my mother-in-law standing next to me, I was sworn in with the Coast Guard Academy Bible that my father-in-law, Walter, had carried with him in the Merchant Marines in World War II. His ship had been torpedoed on a supply mission to our Soviet allies in Archangel, Russia. Walter had clung to his Bible for a week in a lifeboat with fellow survivors in the frigid Arctic waters of the Barents Sea near the Kola Peninsula.

The history of this particular Bible had a big impact on Mike Pence, who kept looking down at it and then up at my mother-in-law as I told the story.

We chatted awhile, and I told Vice President Pence that my home is near the U.S. Naval Observatory, where vice presidents have their official residence. As we chatted, I told Pence that with my younger son wrapped up in high school activities, Kristie and I were spending a lot of time with our dogs, a golden retriever named Duchess and a bearded collie named Rosie.

"Oh, I love dogs," Pence said. "Bring 'em over, the residence is all fenced in like one big old dog park." The idea of using One Observatory Circle as a dog park made Kristie and me chuckle. I was touched by the vice president's offer, but I didn't take it seriously until I received an email from the vice president's assistant with instructions to clear our names with the Secret Service so our dogs could, in fact, run around the Naval Observatory.

I often think back to other interactions with Mike and Karen Pence, how decent and normal they are. Like millions of other Americans.

★ ★ ★

Once I was chair of the Council of Economic Advisors, I was free to speak. I often appeared on CNBC, CNN, and Fox. Why was I the only member of the Trump administration who was a regular on MSNBC? It is my nature to want to constructively engage people who disagree with me. President Trump told me that he appreciated my frequent appearances on television. He loved it when his people were "strong" and articulate in defending the administration on television.

On November 17, 2017, he saw to it that I was asked to take the lead in the daily briefing in the James S. Brady Briefing Room of the White House. Press Secretary Sarah Sanders turned the podium over to me, and I took questions on negotiations with key senators on the president's tax cuts. I was asked by one reporter why we were engaging in "trickle-down economics" when it hadn't worked before. The question was more than a bit snarky. The presumptions of the media lean hard against traditional economics, adopt the tropes of the Left, and are always in the direction of the Drift. I replied that the "fact is that countries around the world have cut their corporate rates and had broad-based reforms, like we're doing on the individual side, and then seeing economic growth result . . . in every economic model I've seen, you get growth—either a lot of growth, or sometimes if it's a closed economy model, a little growth. But you get positive growth out of this. And that growth will benefit workers. . . ."

As in my Senate hearing, I didn't repay a hostile question with a hostile response. In the White House briefing room, I relaxed on stage, made a few jokes and fell into a comfortable conversation with the White House press corps. The president appreciated my effectiveness before a microphone and came to respect me all the more and to rely on me for advice on a wide range of topics.

Defusing hostility is not an inborn talent but a learned skill. As I write these words now, I wonder how history might have changed if this had been a skill Donald Trump himself had managed to master.

## CHAPTER THREE

# Showboats and Human Torpedoes

A fter the *New York Times* published an op-ed by "Anonymous" entitled "I Am Part of the Resistance Inside the Trump Administration," Never Trumper Bill Kristol guessed on Twitter that I was Anonymous. Like many pundits, Bill couldn't understand how a traditionally conservative economist like me—a former advisor to John McCain and Mitt Romney—could work for a protectionist-populist like Trump.

But I was not a secret Never Trumper. I am a mainstream economist, but many of my peers with their models focused on the dire consequences of an all-out trade war, didn't get Trump. They tended to miss the forest of Trump's strategy and obsess over the single tree of a tariff, or the threat of one.

What was that strategy? When Trump announced a new tariff (and sometimes it was only an announcement), he was seeking leverage. The goal in all cases was not trade war but a new and better deal. Compared to the record of his predecessors, it was unconventional. It rattled a lot of people, but it worked.

These were just some of the lessons I was learning about Trump as I met with other members of his senior economic team in the West Wing's Roosevelt Room where the team also met, often with the president, for Tuesday meetings on trade. This venue is one of the most storied rooms in the White House, displaying Theodore Roosevelt's Nobel Peace Prize on a mantle, oil portraits of TR and his relative FDR, furnished with reproduction Chippendale and Queen Anne chairs. It was a decorous setting for some of the most indecorous arguments, I am sure, in White House history.

The meetings were a free-for-all. Some on the team, such as my eventual close friend Peter Navarro and Wilbur Ross, were all-in on tariffs. Others, such as Gary Cohn and yours truly, believed they would do more harm than good. Trump loved it when the two sides argued, and the arguments got very, very heated at times. "Globalist asshole," Peter Navarro, the president's trade advisor, said to me more than once in that hallowed room. When I presented a chart that showed that the cumulative tariffs we were proposing were bigger than the famed Smoot–Hawley tariffs, and about the same size as the 1828 "Tariff of Abominations" (which almost started the Civil War several decades early), Peter shouted, "This chart is fucking unprofessional," at me. Peter is a genius at getting under people's skin, but he usually failed to do so with me. That time though I lost my cool and rose out of my chair. Chris Liddell, an assistant to the president, was worried enough about what might happen next that he physically restrained me. Things calmed down right away, and Peter and I laughed about the dustup together a few moments later.

When the president wasn't with us, our arguments might have been heard by him in the Oval Office across the hall. If so, I am sure the president didn't mind it. What he minded, actually feared, was getting snowed by Washington groupthink, the very thing he had run against. He wanted trade warriors such as Peter Navarro, Steve Bannon, and top aide Stephen Miller to provide the impetus for change. But he also knew that sweating the details was not their strong suit. He wanted a traditional economist to provide detail and a reality check.

I used to teach a class on government at Columbia University, and when I did, I would ask students to define the problem of governing. After much discussion, I would hit them with my definition. The problem with being president is you have to make decisions every day about things that you have never thought about before. You need to have advisors who know the details intimately. But, since they know the issue better than you do, you never know if they are lying to you. The problem of governing is making good decisions when everyone around you might be lying.

Trump solved that problem by genuinely building a team of rivals. By the time Peter Navarro and I were done arguing things through, the president had a pretty good idea of the truth.

Gary Cohn had filled my role while I was awaiting confirmation. His knowledge is deep, but Gary was a financier, not an economist. He was relieved when I stepped in to provide technical expertise and replace him as "the globalist asshole" in the Roosevelt Room. My appearance reassured Gary that balance would continue in the White House's internal trade debate, leaving him to dedicate his talents to enacting administration policy.

When policy was vetted and agreement reached, the arguments might resume in the Oval Office in front of the president. I saw that Donald Trump was smart and capable of moving very quickly, willing to overrule his close advisors when another provided an irrefutable fact that made one proposal or another unworkable.

In time, my sparring partners, Peter Navarro, Steve Bannon, and Stephen Miller in particular, came to see that I wasn't there to derail the president's reorientation of trade but to make it realistic and workable. And despite the tough moments, we all became friends. Almost every day, Peter would swing by my office, sit on a comfy couch, and shoot the breeze about the day's happenings. I even practiced aikidō with him at times in the office. Before he left the White House, Steve Bannon often invited me and Peter over to his office to chat things through. He would pop into my office as well. Just to mess with their minds one day, I arranged for a giant globe to be delivered to my office. When Steve or Peter stopped by to talk, they got to look at the globalist asshole's globe right there on the top of my desk.

* * *

Inside the White House, I could see substantive (if not exactly calm) work being done on reorienting U.S. policy. Outside, it often looked like a zoo.

One day I was in one of Gary Cohn's National Economic Council meetings when a man wearing sunglasses inside the White House—who does that?—popped his head in and said hello. It was Anthony Scaramucci, Harvard Law grad and one of Gary's Goldman Sachs alum friends. He walked in, visitor tag swinging from his neck, and plopped into a chair to take in the discussion.

It turned out that Anthony was waiting for his clearance to become the new White House communications director. His brisk, assertive, and sometimes insulting manner drove then press secretary Sean Spicer and others to resign in protest. But I loved him immediately. Why was Anthony chosen by the president? Because Anthony is very good on television and is smart as a whip. He was almost certainly told by the president to undermine and help eject the president's chief of staff, Reince Priebus, who was proving to be too mild-mannered for Donald Trump's taste. Scaramucci accomplished his mission with all the subtlety of a human torpedo. It is, of course, in the nature of torpedoes to destroy themselves as well as their targets. His White House tenure lasted ten days, hence that eponymous unit of time. I remember Anthony's being at one White House senior staff morning meeting held in the chief's office. He stood in the back corner and watched quietly, never uttering a sound. At the time I thought he was playing it smart, not wanting to showboat before he got the lay of the land. He might be a wild man on TV, I thought, but he is a serious strategic player.

Anthony and I would become friends, and we remained friends even after he turned on Donald Trump as the reelection approached, meeting for dinner at his restaurant in New York City. He had served his role as a change agent, helping to replace Priebus with John Francis Kelly, former Marine Corps general and secretary of Homeland Security. If Priebus had the calm, deliberative demeanor of a college dean (who didn't mind attending frat parties), Kelly was a stern Jesuit teacher entering an elementary school class that had been left to itself for too long. Always at his side was Kirstjen Nielsen, his deputy from Homeland Security, who stepped into the maelstrom and began to impose order as the deputy chief of staff.

Kelly hated disorder and its agents, whom he identified as Steve Bannon and Anthony Scaramucci. Kelly and Nielsen were especially concerned about the unstructured way both advisors had slipped information into the president's hands, disrupting the organized flow of information that normally defines a presidential administration.

From then on, we had a more organized, disciplined way of vetting information and refining options for the president. This would begin, Kelly told us, with senior staff meetings. Where would those meetings be? I sent an email to Kirstjen asking for the venue. An email shot back from her to me, "Why the fuck am I getting emails like this?"

A quick scan of Kirstjen's email told me it was meant for her assistant and was accidentally sent out to me. In short order I learned that she was gracious but tough, and just wanted the trains to run on time. No matter, this was like the U.S. Marine Corps, and people spoke like that in the Corps. The important thing was stuff got done.

John Kelly and Kirstjen Nielsen were what the Trump White House needed—wartime consiglieres.

Early on I met with the new chief of staff to brief him on the role of the CEA, its powers and responsibilities under the 1946 Employment Act. Then I took a risk with my new boss to make a personal aside, "General, I am not a needy person. I'm here to help everybody be successful. If you ever need to set up a meeting and you don't feel like you need to invite me, I'm never going to sweat it."

He stared at me in silence for the longest time. I may be the first person in the history of the White House to ever say something like that to a chief of staff. Senior staffers are always trying to edge around one another to get into the big meetings, like jungle plants trying to push rivals aside for the sunlight. And here was someone who didn't need that drama and wasn't going to complicate the chief of staff's day by begging for attention.

Months later, Kelly and I were next to each other on the ellipticals in the White House gym. He looked at me and said: "The smartest thing anybody ever said to me in this White House was that time you told me you don't need to be in every meeting. Almost everybody who goes into the Oval Office regrets it."

In our meetings with the president, I began to take notice of body language. More than once in an Oval Office meeting, if I had something to say front and center, Vice President Pence would get out of his chair and give it to me. That's the kind of gentleman he is. Peter Navarro paced and showed up with giant visuals in the Oval so often that I began to think of him as being like the guy outside a business that is twirling an advertising sign. Priebus had been a hovering presence. But Kelly stood in the back of the Oval, on the opposite side of the room from the president's Resolute desk, arms folded, watching over the proceedings. Kelly was not concerned with chiming in with his opinion, although he had a good grasp of the issues. His concern was that the president benefit from a rational and orderly sorting of advice. And if this meant standing by the president like a bouncer, he was more than happy to play that role.

And so Kelly imposed structure and order on the White House staff.

With Kelly's boss, however, there was clearly a conflict. John Kelly was a man who had spent his career heroically leading combat troops with military discipline. He told me a story once of how he was riding around Iraq one time on a very hot day when he saw a group of Marines sitting under a tree to grab the little bit of shade they could find. He sensed danger and told his driver to stop the car. "Don't you understand you guys are bunched together and sitting ducks, spread out," he told them. A little bit later, he said, his voice dropping to a whisper, those heroes were hit by an attack. Kelly came from a profession in which discipline was the difference between life and death. Imagine how frustrating it must have been for John Kelly to enter the world where the president who came to Washington to be a disruptor would at times adhere to normal order, but then go off on a tweetstorm and make impulsive decisions. Kelly imposed order on the White House staff, but the disruptor-in-chief was pursuing a strategy that was antithetical to Kelly's military traditions.

We could all feel the tension. Day by day, I could see Kelly's patience wearing thin with the president, and the president's tiring of being corralled and contained by his chief of staff. We all knew that Kelly was absolutely necessary and that he wouldn't last.

\* \* \*

At times I saw the downside of generals thrust into civilian jobs.

Once, at a meeting at the Trump National Golf Club in Bedminster, New Jersey, the senior staff prepared for an important discussion on economics. A closed-circuit television was set up to loop in senior staff in the White House from the situation room. About half the team was in New Jersey, and half the team was in the White House. There were many things to discuss, including breaking developments from around the world. Before the meeting began, I looked around me and saw every face made famous from those years in the White House. On the other end, I saw Jared, Ivanka, Rob Porter, the staff secretary who was always with the president, and other top White House officials. Chief Kelly walked into the situation room and ordered us to start the meeting. People in Bedminster began to talk, but we couldn't hear them. The technology did not work for some reason. We couldn't hear our colleagues.

"This is fucking unacceptable," Kelly said, and promptly ended the meeting.

The rest of us were more than willing to wait for IT to fix the problem. The meeting was important. We had all prepared. The abrupt cancellation cost us. But generals who tolerate screw ups like this can get troops killed. They just can't bear them.

Another time, Defense Secretary Jim Mattis, another four-star like Kelly, was brought to the chief's office to go over breaking developments in Venezuela. Gary Cohn asked me to discuss the economic implications if Venezuelan oil were to stop being exported. I spent a long night estimating the impact on oil prices and gasoline prices. In the southeastern United States, Venezuelan oil was far more important than I thought, and I had some very informative visuals prepared for the group in the chief's office.

"Why the fuck are we talking about economics?" General Mattis asked.

The room went silent. The economic dimensions of Venezuelan oil affected the Iran sanctions, the potential for Russia or China to get more involved in Caracas, and the direct energy security of the United States. How could a general not see the geopolitical implications?

Some senior corporate executives also seem at sea when they enter government service. Secretary of State Rex Tillerson skipped the consequential White House meetings on tariffs and trade policy that were stress tests with so many allies. He had little presence in the White House and even less to say. I attended countless meetings where he was present but can't remember his ever speaking. The former ExxonMobil CEO seemed to fill his time trying to make the State Department a more efficiently functioning organization. It was like hiring a conductor who steps down into the orchestra pit to make sure all the strings are tight and the brass is polished. But he didn't appear to play an instrument himself, at least not in front of the rest of us.

Tillerson, Mattis, and Kelly represented a distinct stage in the Trump White House. Each had his limitations. But they did provide the order needed to plan and execute effective new policies. Looking back, they were like general contractors who came in to get a building project that had gone sour back on schedule. But once the building was built, it was time for them to move on.

★  ★  ★

As I settled into the White House, I got to know the personalities of the Trump White House, from the quiet and effective to the showboats and characters. I made a habit of asking everyone to come over to the CEA and meet with the staff at one of our morning meetings. Almost everyone did. This accomplished two goals for me. One, it made the CEA staff really understand that they were in the middle of "the show." I think the occasional all-nighters were easier to take for my staff because they knew they were in the loop. It also introduced the staffers, who were impressive people in their own right, to the rest of the White House. Joel Zinberg, for example, is a famous cancer surgeon who has practiced in New York City. He also has a law degree from Yale Law School. Joel handled legal issues for CEA but was also in the middle of our health policy team. While the image of the Trump team that one acquired from outside might be that it was made up of hacks, there were a larger number of White House staffers of Joel Zinberg's quality and reputation.

One visitor to CEA who was a big hit was Omarosa Manigault Newman, well known as one of the stars of Donald Trump's hit reality TV show, *The Apprentice*. She often sat next to me in senior staff meetings and was glad to come over and meet my team.

She was an assistant to the president and director of communications for the Office of Public Liaison but was really a free-floating agent within the White House. In December 2017, Kelly fired her for misusing the White House car and driver pool and other "money and integrity" issues. That might have been just an excuse. Kelly bristled at the way Omarosa ignored the White House protocols, and he talked at times with a few of us about how seriously he took her offenses. For example, it is a classic alpha move to have your assistant interrupt a meeting with someone. It makes whomever you are meeting with feel less important than you. Omarosa had her assistant interrupt Cabinet meetings in order to hand her notes. Things like that drove the good general crazy. Whatever the truth of the abuse accusation was, Kelly was irked enough to want her gone, and he made it happen. Interestingly, there were other people, such as Navarro, that Kelly wanted to let go, but the president wouldn't let him. If someone left, it only would have happened because the president signed off on it.

Omarosa told us that she had grown up in public housing and had suffered from asthma as a child. My chief of staff, D. J. Nordquist, and I admired the way she had pushed to remove lead from public housing. She was always gracious, friendly, and engaging with me. When she left, I missed her, just as I did Spicer and Scaramucci. One of the things we began to notice was that there tended to be surprise departures on Fridays. My chief of staff began to call that day of the week "Fry-day." Fry-days were very taxing emotionally because despite the apparent chaos, a community of close friends was gradually taking shape. D. J. used to start sentences with, "In a *normal* White House…"

Jared Kushner and Ivanka Trump both proved to be calm, low-key, and effective. The president's oldest daughter is a policy nerd who filled in the substance on many of the president's banner policies. A *cum laude* graduate in economics from the Wharton School of the University of Pennsylvania, she often asked me for advice on labor economics to guide her work in devising apprenticeship and job training policies and promoting global entrepreneurship for women. More than once she sent a draft back reminding me to include a paper or statistic I had missed. From cities across the United States to India and Germany, Ivanka's appearances followed a predictable pattern. Her public engagements were always preceded by attempts to cancel her and snarky comments about American "royalty." When she presented, though, people couldn't help being impressed, as all of the nerds in the White House were. When

Ivanka appeared with Chancellor Angela Merkel and International Monetary Fund Managing Director Christine Lagarde, *Bild* reported she had made "a sophisticated and level-headed impression."[1] She was probably the smartest person in the West Wing, and because of that, the president trusted her more than anyone.

Jared displayed a talent for winning the trust of corporate executives, NGO leaders, members of Congress, and heads of state. He tended to take on huge problems and calmly cut through the red tape to get things done. Though he was dismissed by the Beltway media as a nepotistic interloper, I saw firsthand how effective Jared was in cementing the blocks for a solid foundation for some of the more substantive achievements of the administration, from sentencing reform to the Arab–Israeli peace deal to immigration reform. Jared was the brains behind the emergency actions during the COVID crisis that got ventilators to those who needed them and designed a vaccination development program that created a race amongst private companies rather than a centrally planned bet on one horse.

Joe Hagin, White House deputy chief of staff for Operations, who had been a longtime aide to the first President Bush, was another advisor of great substance. Early on I was blocked from the executive gym and parking on West Executive Avenue, the closed-off street between the Executive Office Building and the White House. It may sound petty, but when you're putting in sixteen-hour days, anything that saves time means a better chance of spending at least a few minutes with family before going to bed. Joe understood that as chairman of the CEA, I was equivalent to an assistant to the president and should have access to these facilities. He let me in.

Peter Navarro was always the most colorful of all the substantive characters. Harvard Ph.D. and author of a number of books, including the prescient *Death by China*, a polemical book and now documentary. *Death by China* struck many as one-sided and hysterical when it was published in 2011, but it sounds like a fair description of reality a decade later. Peter and I exchanged views almost every day at the end of the day, but I came to know and like Peter during the campaign when he asked me to brief him on the border adjustment tax for candidate Trump.

Up until the Trump administration, the United States was generous in setting favorable trade terms in order to secure good relations with needed allies. We opened the door to China, believing that generosity on our part would lead to the development not only of a rich China, but a more pluralistic, if not democratic, one. What constituted good policy in the early Cold War period, however, had become a policy on autopilot.

It was Peter's observation that allies had taken advantage of stupid U.S. negotiators. We got many details wrong and never came back when our trade partners took advantage of our goodwill.

Peter saw South Korea as the first test case. He was right that U.S. negotiators simply never looked under the hood on this deal.

When the George W. Bush and Barack Obama administrations negotiated with the Koreans, it was agreed that both countries would open their car markets. The Koreans agreed to allow American car companies to sell cars under the U.S.–Korea Free Trade Agreement. But there were problems: Korean rules made it hard for American dealerships to make money by selling service plans. They imposed safety and environmental rules that discriminated against American cars. The South Koreans also imposed rules to report to the consumer routine and minor reconditioning of vehicles after shipping that made American cars seem damaged. As a result of their market distortion, the streets of America are full of Hyundais and Kias, but Chevys and Fords remain a rare sight in Seoul.

In the renegotiated deal, President Trump won concessions from South Korea on rules that restricted U.S. car sales, as well as voluntary restrictions of steel exports, and fair treatment for U.S. pharmaceuticals.[2] I began to learn that Navarro was on to something.

As I began to dig into our trade deals, I could see Peter and the Trade Warriors were often right. But they also overlooked important details. Yes, there was a big disparity between U.S. tariffs on German cars, and German tariffs on U.S. cars. But Germany did agree to make major investments in the United States, with Mercedes, BMW, and Volkswagen building and operating enormous car plants in the American South. BMW not only made 355,000 cars in the United States in 2018, its Spartanburg, South Carolina, plant also exported more than 102,000 "German" cars to Germany, China, and Europe, reflecting money invested in American jobs that boosted American exports.[3]

Overall, though, I came to agree with Peter on trade policy. Our trade deals were riddled with lopsided terms. These terms reflected the priorities of American foreign policy planners, not good economic sense. Many such deals were holdovers from a desire to placate and strengthen allies to stand by us in taking on the Soviet Union. Had anyone noticed that the Cold War ended decades ago? Or that we weren't as big as we used to be, either?

In 1987, the United States produced almost 30 percent of the world's goods and services. With the rise of China, India, and the globalized economy, our share in 2018 was just above 20 percent. In the meantime, the People's Republic of China had zoomed to 19 percent.[4] From 1970 to 2015, the U.S. economy grew threefold, but the total value of goods and services traded internationally increased nearly eleven times.[5] We didn't grow as much as the world did.

As the Trump administration sought to rebalance trade deals, the president had no lack of authority to use tariffs and import restrictions to secure the undivided attention of our trade partners. In dealing with foreign countries, the president acted for the first time in fifteen years to follow up on "201" cases. In these instances, U.S. makers of crystalline photovoltaic solar panels and large residential washing machines claimed they were unduly harmed by import competition. When the investigations were complete on these 201 cases, President Trump levied new import restrictions.

Another presidential power he used came from Section 337 on infringement on patents, trademarks, and other intellectual property. At least twenty 337 cases have been completed since January 2017, and an additional fifty-one are underway. Section 301 of the Tariff Act of 1930 allowed the president to impose remedies against unfair methods of competition and importation, another arrow in Trump's quiver.

When he imposed a tariff, President Trump often took trade partners by surprise. This was by design.

"Kevin, this is the same thing I did in real estate," he said. "If I was having trouble closing a real estate deal, I would sue the guy if he didn't give me what I wanted. A threat to sue would have had no effect. But if I sued him the day before closing, and then offered to withdraw the lawsuit as part of the deal, they almost always signed. They knew you meant it."

He renegotiated bad deals that disadvantaged American workers with this approach. Threatening tariffs had little impact compared to actually imposing tariffs and *then* negotiating.

This ability to pressure the other side was the reason why Donald Trump preferred bilateral trade deals to multilateral trade deals like the Trans-Pacific Partnership. "You're never going to make progress if you have to negotiate with ten countries at the same time," he told me. Instead, he preferred to make a great trade deal, a model deal that the administration could then point to with other countries as the place we both needed to get to.

## CHAPTER FOUR

# The Forest and the Trees

T rade was the trickiest part of my job throughout my time in the White House. All economists agree that free trade, in the abstract, is a good thing. But I must admit, Donald Trump challenged and updated my thinking on how trade, in concrete terms, is practiced. Just as American statists impose strangling regulations on the capitalist economy and then assert that any bad news is cause for more government, they also negotiate trade deals that disadvantage American workers and move jobs overseas, again undermining support for capitalism. Asymmetric trade deals are, Donald Trump recognized, an important contributor to the Drift. I was tossed into this maelstrom from the beginning. My first day on the job, in early June of 2017, started with a short meeting with Jeremy Katz, the deputy director of the National Economic Council. Jeremy took me into his office in the West Wing and said, "Thank God you're here. The president has been presented with an endless stream of economically illiterate analysis. We need a real economist." Katz was right. While Peter Navarro and the rest had a lot to teach me about how asymmetric and disadvantageous our trade deals were, they also got some stuff wrong, which at times locked incorrect ideas in the head of the president.

For example, during the campaign, Peter Navarro had penned a paper with Wilbur Ross, who went on to become secretary of Commerce. One economist called the Navarro–Ross paper "a complete mess," with liberal writer Matthew Yglesias adding that that characterization was "too kind."[1]

The paper asserted that the curtailing of any import would automatically lead to a concomitant and equal increase in U.S. economic growth. Eliminating the trade deficit the United States then had of $500 billion would mean an automatic $500 billion in domestic growth. With labor constituting 44 percent of our national economy, such a move would pump $220 billion in added wages.

This would be wonderful if it were true. In fact, if it were true, no nation on earth would have a reason to trade at all. But it was based on unrealistic assumptions.

Navarro's idea was that if tariffs make it too expensive to buy a $100,000 Mercedes made in Germany (assuming it wasn't made in Alabama), the consumer will buy a Ford, which adds to U.S. economic growth. But what if the higher cost prompted the consumer to stay in her old car a few more years? What if the cost prompted her to buy a cheaper Toyota and swallow the proportionally lower tariff?

The Trade Warriors had somehow unlearned the concept of comparative advantage from the nineteenth century English economist David Ricardo. According to that bedrock principle of modern economics, it makes sense to import wool from New Zealand and export Apple computers back to them. With the United States set to export more oil than we import in a few years, Donald Trump often wondered why the United States imports petroleum products at all? After all, recent advances in fracking have catapulted the United States to a world-leading position in petroleum production. For example, our legacy refineries were made to process high-sulfur heavy and sour crude from Venezuela, while foreign refiners invested long ago in refining the kind of "sweet" crude that now comes from the United States. Such massive investment makes it difficult to change imports and exports with the wave of a wand.

Once in the White House, I quickly found the president took advice from two wings. The Trade Warriors—Peter Navarro, Wilbur Ross, Stephen Miller, and Steve Bannon—provided the drive to remake U.S. trade but were often as guilty as the trade negotiators of the past of not doing their homework. If the president took every word of their advice, he would have been slapping tariffs like a supermarket clerk firing off price labels.

The other set included practitioners like Gary Cohn and Steven Mnuchin who understood that if you slap tariffs willy-nilly, you will hurt consumers and U.S. businesses large and small. If you put a tariff on steel, it's good for the steel companies but bad for American companies that make bicycles out of steel. If you put a high tariff on French wine, it will help winemakers in Napa but hurt restaurateurs and retailers who sell more expensive wine by limiting their choices. The president loved listening to the Trade Warriors to drive his agenda. But he needed the others to keep him from driving into a ditch.

Peter's aggressive style would eventually get him demoted by Kelly, forcing him to send memos to the president through Gary Cohn. But in the early days, Peter was the entertainment in the White House staff meetings and in meetings before the president. He appreciated that the president's eye was ever on the Americans working in the factories, on the welders, truckers, printers, auto and aircraft mechanics, food service workers, accountants, and others who serviced the manufacturing and industrial sector and kept the nation going. Donald Trump's deep concern for the welfare of Americans in blue collar jobs and small business was heartfelt. And his vision wasn't just limited to the "white working class" that media and pollsters so often pointed to as his base. Donald Trump realized how important these lower rungs of the ladder were to blacks, Latinos, and other minorities. Trump and Navarro imparted their concern for working people to everyone around them.

★ ★ ★

In my very first days I was hoping to duck controversial issues and give the internal opposition to my nomination time to die down. But that approach wouldn't last long. Early on, Gary asked me to do a presentation about the economic effects of steel tariffs at the next weekly meeting of the White House committee on trade policy. So I gathered my staff and told them to put together an honest economic analysis. It showed that the net effect of steel tariffs would be a small negative, because the harm to steel-consuming industries—say, American bicycle or car manufacturers—would be larger than the benefit to steel manufacturers.

The George W. Bush administration had tried steel tariffs in 2002. A Commerce Department report found that the Bush steel tariffs had cost by some estimates 200,000 jobs among non-steel manufacturers. This estimated job loss was more than the total employment of the steel industry, then 187,000 workers.[2] Trade economics is notorious for such unintended consequences.

When I arrived in the Roosevelt Room for my first Tuesday morning trade meeting, most of the biggest names in the administration were already gathered. I was on one side of the table as the presenter. I faced Peter Navarro, Stephen Miller, and Commerce Secretary Wilbur Ross, with Gary Cohn, Treasury Secretary Steven Mnuchin, and others in between. I presented the CEA view that steel tariffs would boomerang and hurt the very kinds of jobs we sought to protect.

Right after my presentation, Miller said with some anger, "The president made it perfectly clear throughout the campaign that he supports tariffs. So I wonder why we are having this conversation. We need to ask ourselves, do we support the president's agenda or don't we? If not, then maybe we should leave."

Cohn replied, "I thought we were here to advise the president. If he just wants to do what he said on the campaign, he can just look in the mirror and do whatever he wants, and we can all go home. Or we could just play a tape recorder from the campaign and have that be the meeting. But that is not what he wants."

Gary was right, and he busted Miller for trying one of the most common tricks used in the White House: squashing debate by claiming that the president has already made up his mind.

Later that day, Gary mentioned that Steve Bannon showed up in the Oval Office for a heated discussion on tariffs in front of the president. Afterwards, I asked Gary why he hadn't invited Bannon to the morning presentation, which was supposed to prep us for the afternoon session before President Trump. Gary said that Bannon never attended any meetings that didn't include the president himself. This was just one of the violations of regular order that would later so offend Kelly and get Bannon fired.

Because of those deep divisions within the committee, and Bannon's disdain for the rest of us, if not personally, then at least on the trade matter, we argued over steel tariffs for months. Each Tuesday morning that summer, we gathered in the Roosevelt Room to have another go at it, debating the steel tariffs along with other trade questions such as imposing tariffs on European autos, exiting NAFTA, and imposing tariffs on China. Trying to pry open the minds of people who wouldn't give an inch was exhausting and frustrating. Nerves eventually frayed as tensions grew.

After almost a year of back and forth, I walked into the Oval Office for the meeting that would finally decide the administration's position on steel tariffs. It was Thursday, March 1, 2018. Clouds covered the Washington sky, and the winds howled ominously outside, with dangerous gusts of up to seventy miles per hour predicted. We were there to discuss a new report from the Department of Commerce, which concluded that imports of steel and aluminum imperil U.S. national security. The report also claimed that the president had authority to impose tariffs unilaterally under Section 232 of the Trade Expansion Act of 1962.

"Kevin, please take my seat," Vice President Pence said. As Pence stood, I took his seat directly in front of the Resolute desk, closest to the president. Around me sat most of the White House senior staff and several Cabinet members. I didn't know it then, but this would be one of Gary's last trade meetings as director of the National Economic Council.

President Trump looked at me. "Kevin, what do ya think? About the tariffs?"

"Sir, the tariffs are unlikely to bring back the steel industry," I said. "They might create a few jobs in steel, sure. But they'll destroy more jobs in industries that rely on steel as an input, because they'll raise the cost of steel." This was the same argument I had made during my first presentation to the Tuesday group. If anything, I was pulling my punches. Being too much of an outlier would lose the argument.

Peter Navarro immediately objected, as he always did. The steel industry, he shouted, was in *big* trouble. If the goods-producing industries had flourished for many decades in America's heartland under high tariffs, his thinking went, restoring those tariffs would, if anything, revitalize heavy industry.

"We campaigned on bringing back steel," Peter shouted in front of the president. "We need to do something big, and we need to do it fast. We'll gain net jobs from the tariffs, and the steel industry will boom. But if we don't act soon, it's too late."

Commerce Secretary Wilbur Ross agreed with Navarro, as he always did. He claimed that the downstream effects on steel-consuming industries would be small and that his department's report proved it. Actually, it didn't.

Under Wilbur Ross, Commerce had put out a report on steel tariffs with a methodology that thumbed the scales to guarantee that the benefits of tariffs would outweigh their costs. It failed to address the loss of jobs in all the American businesses that rely on steel and aluminum. If one of my students had submitted that Commerce Department report when I was a professor at Columbia Business School, I would have been skeptical to say the least.

After a few more comments listing pros and cons, Cohn and Mnuchin sided with me against the tariffs.

"I have to think about defending our country," the president said. "Does anyone in this room believe we could win a major war if we didn't have a steel industry?"

I couldn't argue with that logic. If it genuinely was a national security matter, then the pro-tariff position was defensible, even by my standards.

The president knew that I would not be inclined to favor steel tariffs, which is *why* he wanted me in the Oval Office as he finalized his decision. Then he courteously explained to me why he had to go in a different direction, even though he took my arguments seriously.

One morning, Gary grabbed me in the West Wing hallway and said, "Wilbur and Peter have invited a bunch of steel company CEOs to the Cabinet Room to announce the imposition of steel and aluminum tariffs." This was a surprise to all of us. Around that time, the president had tweeted that "trade wars are good and easy to win."[3] Pundits howled in outrage like a band of coyotes. Navarro did several TV interviews to defend the tariffs. He called the prospect of downstream costs from tariffs "fake news."

Was I disappointed? Sure. But I remembered advice from my friend Gene Sperling, an economist who had held major positions in the Clinton and Obama administrations. "You have to remember that you're not the president," he told me. "Speak up before the decision is made, but afterwards you only have two choices: support the team or quit. If you publicly support a decision that you opposed behind closed doors, that will build trust with your colleagues."

★ ★ ★

The decision to impose tariffs was only the end of the beginning. The captain of the ship of state had chosen our course, but the crew had to navigate the ship around one shoal after another.

For starters, we still had to get into the details of whether to exempt America's allies from the tariffs. The steel industry is a political mastodon in countries around the world, including some of our closest security partners. If we gave no exemptions, these mastodons would rear their heads and pressure their governments to retaliate.

On the domestic side, I knew that the tariffs would hurt consumers and some blue-collar workers—two groups who don't have K Street lobbying groups to represent their interests to policymakers. As we moved into implementing the policy, I considered it the job of the CEA to speak up for them as much as possible. We found that the most efficient U.S. steel producers, the mini-mill manufacturers who melt scrap steel with electric arc furnaces, were much more efficient with a tiny workforce than the traditional steel producers who employed large numbers of people to make steel from iron ore. These mini-mills were more likely to take advantage of the tariffs. But their efficiency meant that they could produce more steel than a traditional manufacturer with a tiny workforce. The net effect on employment would be a lot lower than Wilbur Ross and Peter Navarro expected.

In the end, who was right about those steel tariffs? While we cannot quantify the security benefit of being better able to defend ourselves, we now have early data that sheds some light on the economic impact. It backs up my favorite law of economics: be wary of unintended consequences. It also backs up another law: be wary of all forecasts, including your own.

In the wake of the tariffs, and aided by tax reform, America's steel firms invested in new manufacturing capacity. This was the effect President Trump intended: the U.S. industry increased the amount of steel it could produce if a military conflict necessitated firing all the furnaces. One effect of this increase in steel production capacity, however, has been to reduce the steel prices that drive the bottom lines of America's steel companies. As a result, the 2020 equity values of steel producers were lower than they were before the tariffs, which was certainly not the effect their lobbyists had intended.

Meanwhile, neither the blue-collar employment renaissance pre-dicted by the tariff's boosters nor the economic apocalypse envisioned by opponents like me have materialized. Employment in the steel industry since the imposition of the tariffs is down, but the rate of decline is far lower than that of the Obama years. CEA had forecasted that the steel and aluminum tariffs would cause rates of job destruction in excess of what actually resulted.

Overall, we can probably call this tariff battle a draw, and the president's decision to base it on national-defense concerns a sound one. But the steel tariffs were only the beginning. Within the year, the tariff wars within the administration would escalate as we began to scrub every trade deal.

\* \* \*

The steel quotas interacted with another new tariff on imported washing machines, creating a textbook example of that law of unin-tended consequences.

A little history is in order. In 2006, the Department of Justice anti-trust division allowed the acquisition of Maytag by Whirlpool, among the last large U.S. manufacturers of washers and dryers. The government bought the argument of Whirlpool lobbyists that, given strong competi-tion from South Korea's Samsung and LG brands, Whirlpool's domestic dominance wouldn't harm American consumers. Having won that war, more than a decade later lobbyists from Whirlpool convinced Peter Navarro to start beating the war drums against the South Koreans—the evil bastards—for dumping their washing machines in the United States and putting America's manufacturing base at risk.

This argument upended the whole premise of the FTC's approval of the Whirlpool-Maytag deal. After Whirlpool promised the government it wouldn't gouge customers because of foreign competition, it was now petitioning Peter and the president to slap a tariff on their foreign com-petitors. Whirlpool was engaged in classic rent-seeking behavior, the swampiest of swamp moves.

Worse, these rent-seekers hadn't thought through the consequences of their proposal. Washers and dryers are commonly sold as a unit. So slap a tariff on, say, a Samsung washer, and Samsung will shift much of the cost of the tariff to the dryer, making the increase seem more reasonable.

Whirlpool and the Trade Warriors also never thought through how the washing machine tariff would fare if Trump raised steel tariffs. Since Samsung makes its machines in Korea, it has access to cheaper steel without U.S. tariffs. But Whirlpool is in a market where steel tariffs have raised the price of steel.

The Trump administration started its tariff on imported washers at 20 percent, and then 50 percent after an import quota was exceeded. The result? Economists at the University of Chicago and the Federal Reserve Board reported that the unit price for washers rose $86. Dryers rose $92. Consumers bore between 125 percent and 225 percent of the costs created by the washing machine tariffs. The tariffs brought $82 million to the U.S. Treasury, but raised consumer prices by $1.5 billion.[4]

Some 1,800 new American jobs were created, but at a cost of $817,000 per job.[5]

And how did Whirlpool fare, the would-be monopolist? Its share value tumbled in 2018. I couldn't take satisfaction in the company's executives and lobbyists' learning a very expensive lesson because we all paid the price.

To his credit, the president watched the evidence closely and adjusted his game accordingly. He came to understand that his trade objectives could be met with different policy levers than the ones advocated by the Trade Warriors.

★ ★ ★

From the beginning of his quest for the presidency, Donald Trump promised that he would force Canada and Mexico to renegotiate the

North American Free Trade Agreement (NAFTA) or scrap it. This agreement, the handiwork of the Reagan, Bush I, and Clinton administrations, had largely fused North America into a single economy, enlarging markets and allowing each nation to specialize in its comparative advantages. Now Trump threatened to take a battle axe and cut up that market. When Trump was declared the winner on election night of 2016, this promise became a deep source of anxiety, not just for business and political leaders, but for workers and communities that depend on the north–south axis of trade.

At first, Prime Minister Justin Trudeau was hard to reach, consumed by his obvious distaste for Trump. Mexico had elected a left-wing president, Andrés Manuel López Obrador, universally known as "AMLO," who was completely out of sync with the conservative in Washington who wanted to build a wall and make Mexico pay for it. The political situation threatened to undermine any efforts to reach a deal. The president managed to avoid this would-be disastrous outcome with two elements in his strategy, one tough and the other conciliatory. But it took a crisis to make them work in tandem.

In October 2018, migrants from Honduras, El Salvador, and Guatemala began to gather to start a caravan to the United States. They were welcomed by outgoing Mexican President Enrique Peña Nieto with a program called *Estás en tu casa*, "you're home."[6] He had a legal program to educate and feed these migrants but did not forbid them from heading north. We soon saw images of overflow crowds on top of trainloads full of people heading north.

Fox's Steve Doocy said: "Don't call this a caravan. Call it an invasion."[7] Others in conservative media saw the caravan as a highly organized left-wing effort to break down the borders of the United States. President Trump inflamed the situation by telling rallygoers that the migrants had "criminals and unknown Middle Easterners" lurking among them.[8] Extreme voices picked up on this rhetoric, blaming the organization of the caravan on billionaire Jewish philanthropist George Soros.

When the president threatened to militarize the border and close it, Mexico City began to control the caravan.

President Trump's threats at the time struck many as injudicious, even hysterical. I realized he was pursuing his old strategy of launching a lawsuit just before a real estate closing. He understood how and when to apply pressure for a maximum result.

After the caravan crisis, there were signs the border was still out of control. I attended a meeting in John Kelly's office in spring 2019, to discuss options when President Trump called in from the road and declared, "I want you right now, this moment, because it's a national security issue with all these people coming across the border, to announce to the world that we're putting a 25 percent tariff on everything from Mexico. I don't want anyone to argue against it. I'm leaving, and I want to hear it announced by the time I make it to Air Force One."

Steven Mnuchin spoke up.

"Well, you know, sir, we need at least twenty-four hours to work out the details of how to do that," the treasury secretary said. "We've got to run it past the lawyers, figure out exactly what authority we're going to use. So we'll get right on it, but you can't announce it tonight."

The president nodded, seeming to accept Steven's advice. Leaving us, he emphasized, "I still want it done right away."

I was distraught. A 25 percent tariff would be like hitting the brakes with both feet in a racecar going 180. Mexico would retaliate, of course, and it would be U.S. farmers, factory workers, truckers, and white-collar professionals who'd go through the windshield first. The border crisis was now fully entangled with NAFTA, threatening to sow economic chaos. When asked on CNBC Business if the tariffs could possibly be good for the United States, I deflected: "What would be good for the U.S. economy would be to get the border situation under control."[9]

My wife, Kristie, watched the show and told me she could see the anxiety on my face.

Then, like a hurricane running out of energy, the border crisis dissipated, and the trade deal fell neatly into place.

While using confrontation and threats to initiate a relationship with Mexico, President Trump dispatched Jared Kushner to Mexico and Canada to work out a replacement to NAFTA. Jared's smooth ability to build trust and strong personal relationships with the senior leaders of both countries led to the basis for the USMCA, the United States–Mexico–Canada Agreement. It modernized the terms of NAFTA to the benefit of U.S. workers and farmers. It obtained, for the first time ever, collective bargaining rights for Mexican workers. It included efforts by both countries to clean up ocean litter. And it updated intellectual property and digital commerce in a way that kept China from easily using Mexico as a backdoor to ripping off the United States.

The whole episode revealed all the talents and shortcomings of President Trump: the clever willingness to use brinksmanship and play "bad cop" to obtain leverage, the deployment of Jared and other diplomatic voices to "good cop" a better relationship, and the incendiary public rhetoric which was brilliant game theory, but that often stayed in the public's mind longer than the president's actual achievement.

★ ★ ★

As I won the president's trust, my portfolio broadened into representing him before our major economic allies and partners, including key officials at the European Union, the Organization of Economic Cooperation and Development (OECD) in Paris, and the G7 group of leading nations. I was in constant contact with foreign ambassadors, cabinet-level counterparts, and even heads of state. In every direction I encountered polite skepticism that an economist with a Ph.D. could support President Trump. My counterparts often took it as a given that his trade policies were economically illiterate. I responded politely with facts and data that made the case for the president's economic policies. My foreign counterparts didn't like it, but they respected the fact that the Trump administration saw that foreign governments had fleeced previous American administrations. I explained that his disruptive style was a way to keep everyone off balance to open a path to fresh thinking leading to reasonable compromise. Before Trump introduced tariffs, our trading partners had politely declined when previous presidents had attempted to negotiate more level trade agreements. Trump's approach gave the U.S. leverage, and he used it with great effect.

Many of these diplomatic episodes are not yet public, including some involvement in the UK's Brexit negotiations. My experience underscores the benefits of having a president as strong as Trump. When you make a threat to a foreign counterpart, they should know the threat is credible. I could not imagine having the same effectiveness abroad under any other president.

One of my responsibilities included chairing the OECD's Economic Policy Committee, the organization's steering committee. In Paris, I found myself in thorny discussions with the OECD, which was preparing to recommend that its constituent members, which included the largest economies of Europe, impose a digital services tax. We saw this as a tax on a sector that had been invented in the United States. The giants—Google, Facebook, and Twitter—would get hit hard, but so would hundreds of other smaller and innovative firms.

We prepared a surprise for my sometimes-sanctimonious European friends: if you run the math, the tax on U.S. high-tech firms that the Europeans were planning was similar to a tariff. The OECD meeting happens in a giant room that has a rectangular table around which the representatives sit. There were maybe a hundred people in the room. As chair, I sat in the middle at the front, and controlled the meeting with a bell. After sitting through lecture after lecture about how ill-advised our tariffs were, I presented the case that the countries targeting Google were also proposing a tariff. The room was stunned, but at a breakout session at lunch, representatives of the countries targeting our high-tech firms conceded that the issue was "complicated" and that the OECD should study the matter further. This was a huge victory, because it held off the planned tax-tariffs on high-tech U.S. firms and moved the venue to an organization that had its top meeting chaired by the United States.

One other thing might have contributed to the flexibility shown by our OECD allies.

Everyone in the room was aware that OMB Director Mick Mulvaney was an enthusiastic budget slasher. Before the meeting, Mick had decided to zero out U.S. support for the OECD from the president's budget. I believe the OECD is a forum that helps our country pursue economically sound policies. It is an organization that, by design, had institutionalized a strong U.S. presence. Before I went to Paris, I convinced the president and Mick to release the funding for the OECD. I believe that must have had an influence on getting what we wanted from the conference.

The threat of losing U.S. funding was about as subtle as a Mack truck, but I didn't share that we had worked it out until the end of our meeting. I was learning from the master. I am sure that if this tax had gone through when Donald Trump was president, you wouldn't be able to buy a European-made car in the United States. The Trump administration would have responded to the new tax with tariffs against European goods. But I also offered a way out. I suggested countries wait until an economic report could be prepared on the projected effects of a digital tax. We used the president's tactics, and they were a masterstroke, delaying the implementation of these taxes by years and giving our digital companies and innovators time to make their case in the capitals of Europe. How ironic that President Trump was the best ally the high-tech companies ever had on this issue, given the collision with Twitter and Facebook that was to come.

I also met and stayed in close contact with senior European Union officials in Brussels. I often told these officials that the president was serious about his threats regarding NATO. All NATO countries had pledged in 2014 to spend at least 2 percent of their Gross Domestic Product on defense. Some, like the United Kingdom and Poland, exceeded these requirements. Others, including Germany and France, were barely above 1 percent. The president's call has led to significant increases, though neither Germany nor France has reached its 2 percent commitment. On behalf of President Trump, I emphasized to my counterparts that the president wanted to see them meet their obligations.

It didn't help that the president harped on defense spending until it became a sore point. Relations with Germany were particularly strained. I can understand why someone coming from the American right would be critical of the German Chancellor's moderation, her green policies, and acceptance of illegal immigrants. I think some of Merkel's economic and environmental policies are irrational, but as an American they do me no harm. Somehow, a cult of hatred for the placid and methodical chancellor had arisen among some on the right. This attitude bled over into the president's treatment of Merkel. At a G7 meeting, he fished two pieces of Starburst candy from his pocket, slammed them on the table, and said, "Here, Angela, don't say I never give you anything."[10] One struggles to imagine John F. Kennedy treating Konrad Adenauer in that fashion.

I am fluent in German and spent a happy junior year as a Swarthmore student at the University of Hamburg. I was in close touch with the pulse of German opinion and saw that the president's behavior had made him toxic with a key ally. The president did not recognize that he had reached a point of diminishing returns with his rudeness, making it harder for Merkel to compromise lest she be seen by her constituents as bending to his will.

Merkel's chief economic adviser, Lars-Hendrik Röller, is a good friend of mine. We had been teammates in graduate school at the University of Pennsylvania and had formed a friendship while playing together on our intramural soccer team. Hendrik was a natural athlete. He came to the U.S. on a tennis scholarship and had played against Boris Becker. Our team was unstoppable in the intramural league. All I had to do was pass Hendrik the ball. All these years later, we were stunned to find ourselves in the middle of the U.S.–German relationship, but it was a blessing to have someone so trusted to deal with in Europe. He and I were able to back-channel some of the president's overtures to Merkel to help her see why the asymmetry on autos (with German tariffs on U.S. cars five times that of U.S. tariffs) had to be addressed. If worse comes to worst, I told Lars, the administration could investigate the degradation of the U.S. auto industry as a national security concern. And, by the way, Germany was not fulfilling its obligations to NATO.

I also bounced a lot of ideas and proposals off of our ambassador to Germany, Richard Grenell, who hosted me in Berlin in his astonishing modern office near the historic Brandenburg gate. Grenell has the public image of a feisty warrior, but I couldn't help but notice that every time I met with him in his office, he always had his dog with him and showered it with love.

The president and U.S. Trade Representative Robert Lighthizer continued to threaten tariffs on Germany to soften up Merkel's attitude for an actual renegotiation. This put me in a tough spot. As an economist and head of CEA, I had an obligation to include the likely costs of German (and other European) retaliation for tariffs. As the president's confidant, I understood and agreed with the president's strategy. On my many television interviews, I strove to support the president's strategy while remaining honest about possible effects.

There were lighter moments in my travels. My government-issued smartphone included a direct line to the president and often lit up with a "POTUS" caller ID. The president frequently consulted with me to verify an economic statistic he wanted to include in one of his tweets. Sometimes he just called to check on how to spell something. These calls came at all hours, day and night.

The most "memorable" call came when I was in Dublin. Hassett is a widely shared name in Ireland, an Anglicization of an old moniker that meant "strife" or "discord." (Sounds about right.) Everywhere I went I was embraced just for my name alone, a welcoming feeling for a child of the Irish diaspora. My trip to Ireland was spectacular. I stayed at the U.S. ambassador's luxurious mansion and got to spend time with the then taoiseach ("tee-shuck") or prime minister of Ireland, Leo Varadkar. An openly gay man and son of an immigrant from India, Leo was an interesting sign of how much Ireland has changed. Yet Leo also struck me as Irish to the core. I also appeared on stage with him at an event that discussed the impact of Brexit on Ireland and the United States. Some in Washington criticized Ireland for using low taxes to lure U.S. firms abroad. But my view has always been that America was chasing good American jobs away with stupid policy. Perhaps I went a little bit too far on stage that day, as it made quite a stir in the media when I declared that the U.S. tax code seemed as if it were "written by somebody on acid."

I met and dined with Paschal Donohoe—then Irish finance minister, a top-rate economist, and a wicked raconteur. Paschal was anxious because the United States had imposed sanctions on a Russian oligarch who owned an aluminum plant that happened to be the largest plant in Western Ireland.

"You're going to kill us with your Russia sanctions," he told me. He was worried about the plant's closing and Irish workers' losing their jobs.

"I think you have less to be worried about than you might think," I replied. "If sanctions make the plant's aluminum impossible to export, the Russian will simply have to sell to some lucky Irish investor at a discount. Then you'll be rid of sanctions and will own your own plant."

Paschal, being both an economist and a politician, saw the logic in my argument but realized how much anxiety and pain would be felt by his constituents in the process.

"See what you can do, will you?"

I promised to convey his concern. We did, in fact, manage to secure an exemption for the Irish plant. After discussions on trade policies and the onerous digital tax proposal, we proceeded to a lavish dinner hosted by the American chargé d'affaires at the ambassador's residence. Apparently, it is the custom in Ireland to have the cocktail party after dinner, for at 11:30 at night the whole government entourage announced to me that they were going to repair to Dublin's Gravediggers Pub for "a" pint.

I demurred, as I was scheduled to start doing Irish AM media in a few hours. Nevertheless, they were deep in their cups when Paschal asked me if I knew where the phrase "dead ringer" comes from. I did not.

"There was a lady who died and was buried and her husband, heart-broken, went home shaking the dirt from his hands," he said. "It turned out that she was not really dead and managed to claw her way out of the coffin and to the surface, covered in dirt."

He leaned forward.

"She rang at the door, the husband opened it, saw his dead wife and shut it in a fright. She rang the bell again, he opened it again, and shut it again in a fright. And that's where the phrase 'dead ringer' comes from. When she told the story at Gravediggers, she said there would always be a dead ringer for her husband at the door."

On paper, it is at best worth a chuckle. Enacted by Paschal, with his imitation of the poor frightened husband and the weary woman trying to get into her house, it was hilarious. Maybe their pints also helped.

But with Ireland's top-rated morning news show around the corner and jet lag already working its magic on me, I begged off, no doubt ruining my reputation with Paschal Donohoe for all time as a true son of Ireland.

When I got back to my room I thought of how often jet lag had made my eyes snap open in the middle of the night, even when I was very tired. I wanted to get as much sleep as I could for morning television. So I took an Ambien and set my alarm. I had to be on my game when the eyes of Ireland were on me the next morning.

At 2:30 in the morning, I was awakened by a buzzing noise. It took me a while to realize it was just my phone. I thought about not answering, since I had just taken a sleeping pill, but I could tell it was the White House. I answered. Someone was speaking to me, a voice in a deep well saying my name over and over.

"Chairman Hassett, please hold for the president."

I replied with something that must have sounded at least vaguely like an acknowledgment.

As I rose from the depths of sleep, I began to realize I was speaking with the president of the United States.

I cleared my throat.

"Yes, sir, Kevin here, what can I do for you?"

President Trump quickly asked me an economics question for a tweet then wanted to chat about how great the economic news was. I answered him and tried not to be too talkative, dropped the phone and fell back asleep. To this day, I am not exactly sure what we talked about or what, exactly, I might have said.

Whatever it was, I am sure it was true, as I never heard about the call ever again.

## CHAPTER FIVE

# Standing Up to China

One fall Sunday afternoon, I took my son Jamie to practice some hoops at a leafy public park just north of Georgetown. The park has a concrete court and an old basketball hoop, so we brought our basketball and played some one-on-one and horse for a good hour. I showed Jamie that Dad still had the moves, or at least that's my theory, and one I am willing to maintain without empirical inspection. When we were done, Jamie and I were sweat-drenched and grinning.

During the game, I noticed a middle-aged woman of Chinese descent standing at the edge of the court watching us. At first I thought nothing of it. But she never seemed to look away. She wasn't smiling, as one might while watching a father and son play. Her expression was observant, as if she had nothing better to do than stare at the Hassetts all day long. She also appeared to be looking at the nearby National Cathedral, and taking pictures, but did so from an angle that would have put us in the shot.

When we finished up and took our ball to leave, the woman turned briskly and walked toward a parked car. She looked back at me and slid in the front seat without breaking eye contact. While Jamie and I were getting in our car, I turned and noticed that the woman, now sitting shotgun in the front of the car, continued to watch us closely.

"Jamie, jump in the car quick as you can," I said.

I wheeled off, drove to the end of the Cathedral driveway, made a quick right, and another right, sneaking back around to slip in behind the car and see if it was still there. Oblivious to my move, a man who was invisible to us before because he had been laying down in the back seat rose, walked around to the driver's seat and then drove off with the woman next to him. We followed them in, shall we say, an aggressive manner for a few miles.

Back at the White House, I related this info to a national security official.

"You're not supposed to follow them," he said. "That could cause an incident. You might even get killed."

"Who is 'them'?"

"It's China," he said. "They do this sometimes to senior people when they first onboard in the White House. They want you to notice so you understand they are watching you and can get into your business any time they want."

This reminded me of a discussion I had had with my former colleague at the American Enterprise Institute Jim Lilley. Jim had been the U.S. ambassador to China during the Tiananmen Square massacre, and was, before his death, easily the American who understood China the best.

"They do this kind of stuff all the time," I remember Jim telling me. "They would film our new diplomats when they arrived in Beijing, often breaking into their cars and messing everything up, just to show us who was in charge. It was also amazing how often middle-aged men were propositioned by beautiful young Chinese women."

In the months to come, I would work with President Trump and his senior economic and trade advisors on a number of thorny issues in our trade deals with Mexico and Canada, South Korea and Germany. We found plenty of poorly thought-through clauses and exemptions, concessions made from incompetence, indifference, or fatigue by past negotiators that needlessly relinquished American jobs. We cleaned up those deals as best we could in tough talks with countries with whom we have long ties of blood, culture, and commerce.

China was another story. As a candidate, Donald Trump told a crowd in Fort Wayne, Indiana, that "we can't continue to allow China to rape our country." As president, he tweeted: "China is neither an ally or a friend—they want to beat us and own our country."[1]

It sounded extreme then, even to those of us who were already deeply skeptical of China's state-directed, mercantilist trade and industrial policies. And certainly today, after the ravages of the coronavirus, there is no justification, only evil and idiocy, whenever someone conflates the actions of the Communist Party of China with some American passerby who happens to be of Asian descent and launches a racist attack. At the same time, irrational violence against Asian Americans is no reason to pull our punches in criticizing the actions of the Chinese government, which has hurt every American, indeed, everyone on earth.

When Trump introduced his critique of the People's Republic of China with all the subtlety of a 2x4, he rattled an establishment that had grown comfortable selling out to China. If centrally planned China outperforms free-market America, then it accelerates the Drift. As I settled into trade policy on Donald Trump's White House team, it became apparent that the president was right. Germany wants to get the best deal it can for its carmakers. Mexico wants to sell us more autos and avocados. But China weaponizes trade in a way designed to strengthen its economy, technology, and military at the expense of every American. They want to beat us, steal our intellectual property, and own our country. And they want White House officials who stand up to them to be intimidated, even to the point of trying to ruffle them when they play with their children.

★ ★ ★

In the first meeting on trade I attended in the White House, Gary Cohn advanced a realization little remarked-on at the time that gradually came to dominate our thinking and our agenda. Gary asked if we could afford to launch tough trade disputes with South Korea, Japan, Germany, and Australia at the very time we needed to shore up our allies against the mother of all trade abusers, the People's Republic of China.

"Our focus has got to be 100 percent China," he said, "while we leave everyone else alone."

Whatever our differences with our other trading partners, China was a category all its own. With the opening of China to the West in the twentieth century, Chinese goods were allowed into the U.S. economy under the low normal trade relations tariffs, subject to annual renewals by the president. This slowed China's inroads into America more than you would think, since one failure by a president to renew these rates would have subjected Chinese goods to the drastic Smoot–Hawley tariffs of 1930. This lack of predictability restrained U.S. companies from deep investments in sourcing goods from China.

In 2000, the United States granted China permanent normal trade relations (PNTR), ending the need for these annual renewals. American companies quickly outsourced their goods from China and hollowed out American industries around the country. China became the undisputed workshop of the world.

CEA reported studies showing that domestic job losses from Chinese import competition from 1999 to 2011 were between 2 and 2.4 million, with manufacturing jobs close to half of these losses. Overall, China's accession to the World Trade Organization caused 3.2 million Americans to lose their jobs between 2001 and 2013.

The effect of PNTR was like the introduction of an invasive and predatory species onto an isolated island. Like the dodo of Mauritius, many U.S. industries had weak natural defenses against these new predators, and whole economic and social habitats across the United States were wiped out. Two scholars, Justin R. Pierce and Peter K. Schott, performed a rigorous analysis of the impact of opening the American economy to China with the granting of PNTR in U.S. counties with industries hit the hardest: "We find that counties more exposed to the change in U.S. trade policy exhibit relative increases in deaths of despair."[2] Deaths of despair are those caused by drug overdoses, alcohol-related liver disease, and suicide. More than 760,000 Americans have died from drug overdoses since 1999, most of them due to opioids, including the synthetic opioid fentanyl.[3] Pierce and Schott found no pre-PNTR trend in these U.S. counties that could explain this trend. In other words, the very communities that were hollowed out by PNTR became depressed and desolate communities where deaths of despair rose precipitously.

And who has been fueling this drug epidemic? The Brookings Institution reports: "Since 2013, China has been the principal source of the fentanyl flooding the U.S. illicit drug market—or of the precursor agents from which fentanyl is produced, often in Mexico—fueling the deadliest drug epidemic in U.S. history."[4]

Until Donald Trump secured an agreement to curb the fentanyl trade, Americans could access home deliveries of opioids from limitless supplies on the dark web.

The "carnage" Donald Trump decried in his inaugural address was all too real. Meanwhile, as China was hollowing out America's industrial infrastructure, it was also busy using cybertheft, industrial espionage, and forced technology transfers to steal the crown jewels of American innovation. At CEA, we reported in the 2018 Economic Report of the President that foreign theft of American intellectual property costs the United States as much as $599 billion every year. Europe is also a prime victim. The OECD and the EU's Intellectual Property Office have estimated that the global trade in counterfeit and pirated goods alone cost as much as $461 billion in 2013, 2.5 percent of world trade. China is continuing to pry intellectual property—our hard-won inventions—from U.S. pharmaceuticals, aerospace, computer hardware and software, electronics, medical equipment, chemicals, and automobile manufacturers.

What about the prospect of Americans' benefitting from access to the enormous Chinese market? For some service industries like

Starbucks, which has more than four thousand stores in China, the China market has been a blessing. But while China is willing to let us sell them coffee, they will only buy our technology if we're willing to give them our trade secrets. Companies must enter into Chinese joint ventures with approval processes that force U.S. companies to transfer technology and intellectual property.

And if all else fails, China just steals what it wants. The Chinese car manufacturing sector has many instances in which Western cars—GM, Land Rover, Volkswagen—have been exactly reproduced, down to the last hubcap, with a Chinese brand slapped on them.

The Communist Party leaders in the People's Republic of China now believe they have grown the economic and military power of their country to a position in which they can dictate terms. Offended that Australia called for an impartial investigation into the origins of the coronavirus, China slapped Canberra with a list of fourteen demands that must be met to improve relations. These included asking the democratic government to curb debate in Parliament, to allow Huawei and ZTE to roll out Australia's 5G (despite the fact that every Western intelligence service believes they are hopelessly compromised by Chinese intelligence agencies), and to crack down on think tanks critical of China.

In short, China is demanding that Australia curb its democracy and bow in obeisance to Beijing. "China is angry. If you make China the enemy, China will be the enemy," one of its "Wolf Warrior" diplomats said to an Australian representative as he thrust his list of fourteen demands forward.

China's attack on the economy, health, and future of the United States has been just as brazen and bold. And yet, until 2016, few U.S. politicians were willing to match the scope of this attack with the degree of defiance that it deserved. Somehow, the elites of both parties in Washington were stuck in the nineties, still seeing China as a great business opportunity and ignoring how China's predatory, mercantile trade policies transformed communities across the nation into pits of despair.

Donald Trump deserves tremendous credit for seeing the suffering in plain sight that others managed not to see or to ignore. The counties that had been hit the hardest by China went heavy for Barack Obama, who campaigned as a trade skeptic in 2008. As president, Obama made some noise but did very little on the issue. Donald Trump saw his opening when Obama continued to line up with the Washington consensus to ignore China's theft of American jobs.

China's theft of innovation continues and is becoming highly sophisticated. The Chinese Communist Party offers many eminent American and European scientists prestigious and lucrative academic posts at China's leading universities. Some of the scientists who've taken this deal have found themselves compromised by more than money. Many Chinese nationals who study and work in the United States are encouraged by their government to act as amateur spies, stealing as much intellectual property as they can.

China's willingness to spend top dollar to recruit the best talent from around the world has enabled their country to take the lead in quantum computing. Once fully realized, China will have the ability to encode its diplomatic and military operations in codes that are truly unbreakable. China is already testing quantum communications with satellites in Earth's orbit.

Through quantum computing, the 5G technology of Huawei and ZTE, and artificial intelligence, China plans to dominate the commanding heights of the world economy and geopolitics. It wants to own the backbone of the Internet of Things that will link every appliance in your home, allow for remote surgery and health monitoring and enable self-driving cars. If China gets its way, the very fabric of our lives will be owned, operated, and surveilled by China, Inc. Our access to that mainframe will continue only as long as we stay in their good graces.

At least, that's the plan.

★ ★ ★

As our Tuesday trade discussions centered on China, I worked closely with Trade Representative Bob Lighthizer to use our 301 powers under the Trade Act of 1974 to investigate China's behavior, creating a predicate for President Trump to take action.

This was a dicey proposition. Some White House tariff announcements caused the equities market to drop like a stone, up to 11 percent by one measure we used to assess the impact of tarriff news on markets. Announcements of a trade breakthrough caused the market to soar. Given the deep integration of China in our economy, a wrong word could have devastating repercussions. Our approach had to be deliberate and thoughtful.

The thorny question was, what tariffs to recommend?

Put a tariff on the rare-earth minerals critical to America's technology sector, and we would be raising prices on the 80 percent of those U.S. products supplied by China, as of 2018.[5] Such tariffs would be an own-goal, harming U.S. companies and consumers without providing much strategic benefit.

We started looking for products in which we either had other cost-effective suppliers in the United States or with nations other than China, as well as products in which we were China's principal customer. CEA and U.S. Trade Representative economists went to work to produce this list that I am reliably told caused a panic attack in Beijing. Trump was fighting back, and doing so with an almost nasty sophistication.

Next, we looked to defend our manufacturers in the most egregious cases of mistreatment of American manufacturers. In 2016, domestic manufacturers' market share of photovoltaic solar panels was only 11 percent of the total solar generation hardware market on a value basis. After the initial imposition of anti-dumping and countervailing duties under President Obama in 2013 and 2015, Chinese solar manufacturers offshored to other locations, including Malaysia and Vietnam to get around our tariffs. As a result, the import shares by country of origin changed, but domestic manufacturers remain consistently crowded out.

The Trump trade war against China-made solar panels continued through 2020. China hit the United States, South Korea, and the EU with a 53.50 percent retaliatory duty on polysilicon, a key part of solar cells. In 2017, the administration brought a Section 201 case for the first time in fifteen years, asserting that imports of crystalline silicon photovoltaic cells and modules injured our domestic industry.

Biden's election puts a new president in the middle of the Trump strategy with China. The U.S. trade deficit with China in 2016 was $346 billion. It hit a high of $418 billion in 2018. In 2020, it was $310 billion.[6] Only after the economy fully recovers from the effects of the coronavirus will we know if this reduction is due to the pandemic or to the efficacy of Trump's trade policies.

We at least began to respond. About 500,000 manufacturing jobs were added under President Trump, contributing to a partial recovery of 1 million manufacturing jobs since U.S. manufacturing had reached its low point at the beginning of 2007.[7]

President Biden will have some clear-cut choices to make. He has pledged to spend $2 trillion on renewable technologies. We are still dependent on China for solar power technology, including those finished with components from other countries to avoid U.S. tariffs. Much of the markets' polysilicon now comes from China, with much of it from Xinjiang province, where the geopolitical consulting firm of Horizon Advisory reports that China is using Uighur Muslims as slave laborers.[8] Will President Biden and his climate emissary John Kerry open the U.S. spigot to pay China to make solar panels with slave labor?

The story of trade in the Trump administration for me was one of evolution. I came in as a defender of free trade, as a "globalist asshole," but I learned that our trade deals really had disadvantaged the U.S. When China wasn't busy harassing White House officials playing basketball with their children, they were stealing us blind. It was about time Washington fought against this predatory force.

Peter Navarro has a difficult manner, but he was right about China, and his impact on our China policy was one of the most positive any Trump advisor had on any topic. If Trump had let Kelly fire Navarro, we would not have made so much progress.

As I look back, however, perhaps there was method to some of our madness, a version of what President Nixon called his "Madman theory." Nixon, in a calculating way, gave the Soviets reason to believe he was a bit off his rocker on the theory that this would give him leverage. Gary Cohn worried that the bitterness of our trade disputes with allies would erode our mutual ability to stand up to China. After receiving word that some of the stances that President Trump took were causing some in Beijing to panic, however, it seemed to me that his willingness to get tough with allies was helping to psych them out. After all, if he could be that tough with Seoul or Berlin, how much tougher might Trump be with Beijing?

America's elites, caught in the flow of our own Drift, fail to recognize how irredeemably hostile Beijing is to the American ideal. Going forward, will President Biden rally our allies to protect the world system of trade and democracy itself? Now that America is awakened to the danger of China, we must stay awake. Our determination must be bipartisan. And our resolve must last across administrations.

## CHAPTER SIX

# The Three Percent Promise

My mother was a kindergarten teacher. My father taught English at Greenfield High School in rural Massachusetts. He still lives in Greenfield in the family home I grew up in.

Greenfield, at the confluence of several rivers, has been a center of hard work and industry since the opening of a sawmill in 1690. In the nineteenth century, Greenfield's waterwheels powered a thriving mill town with a large cutlery factory. In my childhood, Greenfield still had the world's largest tap and die operation, which employed thousands. Neighboring Turners Falls, where my mother taught, was almost as prosperous, housing a massive paper mill and numerous other factories along the banks of the Connecticut River.

Today, the building that once housed the colonial sawmill is a "Museum of Our Industrial Heritage."[1]

As I explained in my testimony before the Senate, as I grew up, my town shrank. Families started moving away. Graduates stopped coming home after college. In all of this, there is nothing extraordinary about Greenfield. The history of my hometown is like that of hundreds of other

Rust Belt cities, from Connecticut to Michigan. The advantage of hydro-electric power was no longer that decisive an economic factor.

When I began to study economics in college and graduate school, I always came back to the question, why, in a place where industry had thrived since 1690, did the big plants move away or close? Why did many of the good jobs disappear? And is there something that policymakers can do to restore blue collar jobs and prosperity?

My textbooks had economic models that suggested a simple answer: workers can have high wages if they have high productivity, which is enabled by an ample supply of productive capital. But I saw that what works in models is often defeated by the complexities of the real world. I learned to trust data from the real world over pure theory, as so many of my colleagues went on to do. President Trump didn't spend time thinking about theories, but he was smart and had his nose in the data his entire life. For most of it, he was trying to sniff out a profit opportunity. But now, he was trying to find opportunity to restore profits to firms that create opportunity for ordinary Americans.

For my own part, I wondered if there was something else at work. How do countries with high taxes and regulations compare in employment, income, and growth with those with lower taxes? This was harder to determine than it seemed. I noticed early in my career that the country-by-country data often were not available.

A real-world experiment was underway when I was in graduate school. In 1986, when President Reagan's Tax Reform Act passed, I was then a doctoral student in Alan Auerbach's public finance class at the University of Pennsylvania. For my dissertation, I began working on how these tax reforms would affect business capital spending. Could taxes explain the flight of factories away from towns like Greenfield? The literature was surprisingly sparse, often finding little correlation between tax policy and capital spending, which is another way of saying that taxes had little impact on the economy. Even back then, I saw that the academy seemed all too willing to accept that high taxes have no effect on the economy, all too willing to push a finding that served the Drift.

But Alan and I noticed something funny in the data. Politicians tended to pass Investment Tax Credits in recessions, then let them expire when the recession was over. Investments were 10 percent off during recessions. Investments were lower during recessions than in booms, which created the impression that the Investment Tax Credit had the opposite effect.

When Alan and I looked deeper, we found cause and effect had been reversed in the academic literature. Tax policy, it turned out, had big effects on investment behavior, once you accounted for the fact that a bad economy can itself cause tax cuts. Our first study was among a few that launched a whole literature that employ different methods relying on experimental methods to identify tax effects. At the American Enterprise Institute, I would later help build a large international tax database that made this approach easy to apply and replicate for scholars around the world.

When Alan and I went through this exercise, we saw the data were clear: Countries with lower rates of taxation on average did better in terms of jobs, income, and social progress than high-tax countries. Economists who have studied the effects of taxes over time have developed a consensus: lower marginal tax rates and a broader base increase rates of economic growth and well-being.

When I got to the White House, I found that the president and his economic team all shared my belief that good tax policy is fundamentally about jobs, income, and better lives. It took us time to become effective in the service of this conviction. In the early Trump White House, our team was disorganized and at each other's throats over the details of tariff policy. When we started working on taxes, however, we began to come together as a team. It started with President Trump, who refused to accept weak growth as a "new normal" and called on his team to deliver at least 3 percent economic growth, wage increases for the middle class, and job gains for the American heartland. He believed that jobs that were "never coming back" were going to return if we could just get our policies right. This was a vision and a cause that created camaraderie between the president, Gary, Steven, Peter, and me to build an effective coalition between the White House and Congress.

It is fair to point out, however, that the 3 percent growth forecast has an interesting backstory. The president had promised during his campaign that he would deliver 4 percent growth. During the transition and after I was chosen to be CEA chair, the economic team had regular calls, and I warned everyone that 4 percent growth was simply not possible. Indeed, the mainstream professional forecasters were promising growth a bit above 1 percent. Three percent was, I added, about where we should be if all of Trump's pro-growth policy became law.

When we had the final meeting to set the forecast, Steven Mnuchin announced at the start of the meeting that he had discussed our previous conversations with the president, and that he was comfortable if we built in a 3 not 4 percent assumption into our forecast and urged us to document every single policy it took to get to 3, with individual estimates for each policy. That was a huge relief to the economists at CEA and an early sign that Trump would be easier to work with than I had expected at first.

* * *

Since the birth of the federal income tax in 1913, the top marginal tax rate on individual income has fluctuated from its original 7 percent to a peak of 94 percent during World War II (which might be surpassed in a Sanders or if there is ever an AOC administration), to a post-war low of 28 percent towards the end of Reagan's presidency. In 2017, the top marginal rate was 39.6 percent, somewhere between its historical war-time high and birthweight low.

Reducing this rate would be difficult. Politically speaking, we were practically alone.

For decades, tax reform was a bipartisan tradition. President Kennedy's tax initiative, signed into law by President Johnson as the Revenue Act of 1964, lowered the top marginal rate on individual income from

91 percent to 70 percent. The legislation passed as a majority of Republicans in both houses of Congress joined a majority of Democrats in supporting the legislation. President Reagan's 1986 Tax Reform Act was signed into law when Democrats controlled the U.S. House of Representatives. Bipartisanship has been good for tax reform. And tax reform has been good for America.

While this consensus formed and deepened, government acted as if the opposite had been proven true. While the tax code contained about 400,000 words in 1955, it had reached roughly 2.4 million words by 2016. Not surprisingly, the Office of Information and Regulatory Affairs estimated that it took Americans almost 9 billion hours to file their tax returns—a national waste of time and resources.[2]

Big companies can handle the cost of audits, tax planning, research, appeals, litigation, and filing returns. But these costs fall hard on smaller firms. The disparities of the federal tax code were also surprisingly regional. By allowing U.S. taxpayers to deduct their state income taxes, Washington encouraged blue states like California, Illinois, and New York to become profligate spenders, subsidized by taxpayers in states like Texas, Tennessee, and Florida that practice fiscal restraint.

"This isn't right," the president said to me more than once. "Why should New York get to waste Nebraskans' money?"

President Trump was distinguished from his predecessors in his willingness to aggressively take on the tax code and what it was doing to the fiscal health of states, companies, and millions of families. President George W. Bush's compassionate conservatism centered big tax cuts on families with children. He ignored tax cuts on business. The Bush administration did not recognize that the United States, with one of the highest, least friendly corporate tax regimes on earth, was chasing American businesses overseas—which hurt U.S. jobs. If you care about working families with children, high corporate taxes are indeed relevant.

It is a mark of just how bad the Bush tax policies were that President Obama liked them so much. When he took office, he extended the Bush tax cuts and added only a small increase in the top marginal rate for individuals by 37 percent to 39.6 percent. This tinkering was treated in the media and by Republicans and Democrats on the Hill as the final contest between good and evil. Neither party made a serious effort to change corporate taxes because Republicans, going along with the flow of the Drift, had conceded the debate to the Marxist assumption that cutting business taxes is a giveaway to the rich. The data shows that that isn't true, and President Trump wasn't afraid to do what was right despite the names he might get called.

* * *

Many call economics the "dismal science," but I wouldn't call it a science at all. A science is the study of forces governed by eternal laws of nature which can be verified with experiments. But in economics, many of the underlying "laws" that govern public policy evolve over time. Some of the "rules" I learned in grad school in the 1980s about subjects like inflation and unemployment had to be discarded by the 2000s. And we can't run controlled experiments with huge populations very often. The best we can do is measure what happens after a policy decision is made, compare how different policies work under different times and conditions, and across different countries, and then form a theory about cause and effect.

Economics is a humbling field, or at least it should be. The economists who advised Presidents Bush and Obama should have had the humility to ask themselves: Why were American workers suffering the worst labor earnings in modern history?

President Obama and some of his people had bought into a pessimistic view put forward by the economist Robert Gordon that the global economy may have simply run through the best productivity-enhancing innovations, a trend called secular stagnation. There never again will be, the story goes, an invention as important as the toilet. Huge productivity gains from computing, for example, had flattened out early in this century. "The telegraph in 1844 created instantaneous communications, and we are now elaborating on instantaneous communications," Gordon said. "We moved from the speed of the horse and the sail to the Boeing 707, and we have not gone any faster since."[3]

With all due respect to an illustrious economist whose work has had a major impact on my career, Gordon sounds much like the proverbial nineteenth century thinker who declared that man will go no faster than forty miles per hour. There are many new applications on the horizon—such as the integration of robots, 5G, and artificial intelligence—that show great potential for supercharging productivity. Our administration saw the dip in productivity not as a fundamental development in modern human history, but as a failure of policy, a collapse of optimism. Secular stagnation was just the excuse failed economists and politicians ginned up to explain their failure. It was Jimmy Carter all over again.

We at the CEA had a competing theory. We thought that the increasingly complex regulatory environment and tax code were responsible for the loss of robust growth. Like newspaper lining the bottom of a birdcage, the U.S. tax code had accumulated a lot of junk. But the leading economic superstars of the early twenty-first century saw it otherwise. As Washington tax policies became entrenched, a generation of academic economists cobbled together theories that validated Democratic politicians and their increasingly left-wing ideology. Drawing on shoddy analysis and misconstrued empirical data, these liberal economists provided the politicians the ammunition they needed to raise taxes and play the class warfare game while pretending their policies helped the economy. And then when the economy stagnated, they blamed it on some mystical external force, "secular stagnation." American progressives began more and more to drift into Soviet-style thinking: If our policies aren't working, there must be some external force thwarting us. It can't be our basic ideology. President Trump would have none of it.

When discussing corporate taxes, President Trump often made points analogous to our trade discussions. The U.S. was being outsmarted and outmaneuvered by our competitors. Our trading partners were smarter and less ideologically driven than we were. The OECD average of leading countries saw their corporate tax burden decline from 32.3 percent in 2000 to 23.8 in 2017.[4] But the U.S. rate only declined from 39.3 to 38.9 percent, and most of that was driven by reductions at the state level.[5] Meanwhile businesses and jobs were abandoning the U.S. in droves, landing in the places with the lowest tax rates. Despite that, the Democrats and their pet economists were in denial.

During the Obama administration, U.S. firms became less productive. Investment in the United States fell. And the cost of this lower output has been increasingly and disproportionately borne by the less mobile factor of production—namely, labor. In other words, people and their families.

Corporate taxes were key. In this young century, the United States went from being the developed economy with the seventh highest corporate tax rate to the highest in the OECD, and fourth-highest in the world. The other developed countries had a top statutory corporate tax rate of 24.2 percent. In comparison, the combined U.S. state and federal top statutory corporate tax rate was 38.9 percent.[6]

In one meeting in the Oval Office with the president, I described the impact our tax code was having on capital investment, productivity, and GDP.

"This is nuts," President Trump said to me. "But I don't want to talk about GDP. I want to talk about wages, because that's what matters to people, the money they take home. What does our plan do for workers?"

I told the president that if we got tax policy right, the average American family would have between $4,000 and $8,000 more dollars in their annual budget.

He winced a little. You might think that Donald Trump would instinctively go for the higher number. But he had better PR sense than I did. True or not, the president recognized that we would be leading with our chins if we went with the higher number. (On another occasion, we told the president that under his administration,

500,000 jobs had been created in a given sector. He later told the press it was 609,000. When I asked him about it, the president implied that giving the fact-checkers something to correct only served to get the media to agree to the right number, which was smaller but still impressive. I was not appalled . . . but enchanted by his ability to come up with a number that was both imaginary and highly specific—not 600,000, but 609,000!)

So it was with the income figure, but this time his instincts were to downgrade the number.

"When you go on TV, Kevin, I want you to stick to $4,000," the president told me. "Let's under-promise and over-deliver."

I went to work with the economic team in the Roosevelt Room—supported by policy experts at Treasury and CEA—to flesh out what would become the Tax Cuts and Jobs Act of 2017. We acted on four goals in a unified plan that the president had articulated for the TCJA: tax relief for middle-income families, tax simplification for individuals, economic growth through business tax relief, and repatriation of overseas earnings.

We crafted a plan to reduce individual income taxes. We raised the standard deduction, liberating more lower-income Americans from paying federal income taxes at all. We proposed to shave income taxes for middle-class Americans by as much as 4 percent.

On federal corporate taxes, we proposed to reduce the top marginal tax rate to 21 percent and to allow firms to fully expense investments in capital.

Then we made our projections on what this would mean. A U.S. federal corporate rate reduction from 35 to 21 percent would likely result in growth in national economic output by 2 to 4 percent over 10 years and those wage increases for U.S. households of $4,000 or more over 3 to 5 years.

That's serious money for living expenses, for groceries, car payments, tuition, or savings. We were setting out to give the working people of America a raise for the first time in a decade.

* * *

Corporate tax cuts, vilified by liberals and compassionate conserva-tives alike, were absolutely essential to getting Americans back to work and in better-paying jobs. President Trump had realized that U.S. workers had been substantially harmed by the convergence of two undisputed economic trends. The first was the high and accelerating international mobility of capital; the second was the increasingly uncompetitive nature of U.S. corporate income taxation relative to the rest of the world.

The U.S. corporate tax rate, however, was still stuck in the same place as when the Berlin Wall crumbled almost thirty years prior. Worse, our corporate tax code had features that no other country was stupid enough to adopt. Unlike any other developed country, the United States operated a system of worldwide taxation that taxed U.S. corporations on their net income from any source once it was brought back home. This system encouraged U.S. multinationals to defer reporting their overseas profits, incentivizing them to hold large volumes of cash in their foreign subsidiaries in lower-tax jurisdictions. Other OECD countries instead follow either a territorial tax system, in which corporations are taxed only on income generated domestically, or a hybrid tax system, in which foreign income is taxed only if the foreign country's tax system is significantly different from that at home.

How did this work in the real world? Imagine you're CEO of a soap company in Scranton, Pennsylvania, that sells soap around the country for $1 a bar that costs $0.50 to make. One day, your CFO comes into your office and says, "Let's don't be stupid, Washington is telling us to lower our taxes by moving our factory to Ireland." So you fire your American workers, set up an Irish subsidiary, which then sells the soap to its American parent company for $1.01 a bar. You still sell it in America for $1 a bar.

How does that make sense? At home, your soap company would be losing money, so it would pay no U.S. corporate income tax. But by losing money here, you are actually able to credit today's loss against profits made in previous years. So a tax refund from the United States to your soap company ends up financing the new factories in Ireland. Abroad, your subsidiary would be piling up cash, but being in Ireland, that rate is subject to a low tax of 12.50 percent.

Tax attorneys sold this business model as a smart deal to CEOs across the country. American businesses thus came to hold about $1 trillion in cash overseas.[7] From the CEO's perspective, American tax law was practically forcing the move. From the national perspective, U.S. taxpayers were paying to move American jobs overseas, while further hollowing out American industries. In the days of Kennedy or Reagan, a bipartisan coalition for reform would have easily emerged to change something as stupid as this. In our time, support to fix the corporate tax code elicits angry, demagogic responses from those chanting Marxist themes about giveaways to the rich and kowtowing to powerful corporations.

Some of the most storied and highly valued technology firms were parking their money in low-tax venues like Ireland while paying almost nothing in U.S. taxes. By incentivizing companies to shift their reported income abroad, Americans saw lower levels of domestic investment, less physical and intellectual capital formation, and sagging productivity and wage growth.

All of which meant lost income, diminished prospects, and, when paired with China's unfair trade practices, often shorter lives for many Americans. The Drift was not just hurting the economy. It was stealing life and the joy of life from Americans.

Donald Trump, who ran a multinational business, intuitively understood this. He came into office saying, in effect, "Tear down this rate." Those of us working in the Roosevelt Room were eager to make it happen.

\* \* \*

President Trump endorsed our proposal for a Unified Framework for Tax Reform that drew from elements of his campaign proposals, one that would kickstart the economy with reforms to both the individual income tax and the corporate tax systems.

We proposed reducing the corporate tax rate to 21 percent and giving U.S. corporations an opportunity to bring their mountains of cash home, where it could do some good for Americans.

On the individual side, President Trump's framework lowered the rates. We left the door open for a higher marginal tax rate to ensure that the wealthy would not pay a lower share of taxes than they pay today. And our plan made more low-income Americans eligible for the zero rate.

President Trump's plan retained incentives for home mortgage interest and charitable contributions, but otherwise eliminated itemized deductions in favor of a doubling of the standard deduction. In pursuit of simplification, the Unified Framework repealed personal exemptions and enhanced the child tax credit by increasing its size and raising the income level at which it phases out, a reform that also eliminated the marriage penalty. Those who care for other dependents, like the elderly, would receive a new $500 non-refundable credit. The alternative minimum tax and the death tax would both be eliminated. The idea was to simplify the system, end wasteful tax breaks, and eliminate loopholes. It is a simpler, fairer system that would increase the base and lower rates.

We prepared ourselves to make some bold pledges. The president, Steven, Gary, and I publicly pledged on television and in print that if enacted, our tax cuts would bolster average wages by $4,000 in 3 to 5 years. We also predicted we would restore U.S. economic growth to 3 percent, above the postwar average of 2.9 percent and doubling that of Obama's tenure, or, to abstract from the financial crisis and make the same point, roughly doubling the rate of growth of the last 2 years of Obama's presidency.[8]

While we were devising this plan, Gary Cohn and I talked about the need to help the most depressed communities in the United States. We became excited about creating reduced tax zones to encourage businesses to relocate to inner cities and other distressed communities. Previous efforts to revitalize distressed areas had failed, largely because of how the law had been drafted and implemented by bureaucrats to make them as unworkable as possible.

The caricature of the Trump administration in the media was that we only cared about rich plutocrats and the white working class. Nothing could be further from the truth. At the end of each day, I'd go to Gary's office or he'd come up to mine, and we'd talk about ways to extend a policy lifeline to help predominately minority poor Americans. Gary was fired up as an evangelist for Opportunity Zones and the working poor. We worked hard to make the Opportunity Zone legislation as realistic and workable as possible.

We knew from the start that we would face a large problem. The rule makers at Treasury have never seen a tax cut they liked. Attempts by previous administrations to bring reduced taxes to poor communities had been fatally undermined by flawed rules from Treasury staff. The good news was that we had an unusually high degree of tax expertise in our senior economic team. So we decided to propose that when Treasury wrote a rule to implement our new tax laws, those rules would have to be approved by OMB, then run by the meticulous Mick Mulvaney.

Steven Mnuchin, when he learned of our scheme to put his professional staff on training wheels, was not exactly supportive. After all, any Cabinet secretary worth his salt would defend his own turf. This turned into a struggle between Mick and Steven. The president sided with Mick, saying, the story goes, "That's a really good idea, and you should be grateful for the help, Steven."

Mnuchin wasn't happy, but at least he got to tell his people he tried his best to resist the additional oversight. And, to his credit, he smoothly snapped back into the team and became instrumental to the design and eventual passage of the Tax Cuts and Jobs Act. To this day, there is nobody I respect more from my Trump years than Steven Mnuchin.

It still took innumerable meetings with the Treasury technical staff to write the regulations for Opportunity Zones and other details of the bill so that they would work. In one instance, Treasury staff wanted a rule that an investing business would have to locate 90 percent of its assets in the target community.

This made no sense to me. Suppose you want to take advantage of the tax break by locating your brewery in, say, the poor neighborhood of Anacostia in the District of Columbia. The minute you load up a truck with your first batch of beer for grocery stores and bars in other parts of Washington, D.C., you could be in violation of the 90 percent rule, or at least as soon as your truck full of beer crossed the Anacostia River. The way Treasury would have written the tax rules would have left real estate firms and their fixed assets as the only companies able to take advantage of the Opportunity Zones. And yet, the whole point of the proposal was to create manufacturing jobs that would send goods out of distressed communities and jobs in.

So we rode herd on Treasury rules like these to make them workable. But next we faced the problem of paying for the hole we were putting in the federal budget. Theoretically, a tax break costs the Treasury. Where would we make up the difference?

We searched potential venues for taxation and found a target for the new tax that would perfectly offset the cost of the Opportunity Zones. This would impose a 1.4 percent tax on college endowments that were in excess of $500,000 per student. Harvard University, with $39.4 billion in its endowment or $1.6 million per student, would thus pay an additional $37.7 million in taxes.[9] Perhaps with an eye toward the key role that universities play in the Drift—more on that later—I was more than happy to help Harvard do its part for the poor by helping to pay for a free market policy.

\* \* \*

After we unveiled our proposal, we faced a wind tunnel of opposition cranked up to maximum velocity.

I realized how fierce it was going to be when I went on Fareed Zakaria's show on CNN to tout our plan. Fareed began our segment by noting that Larry Summers, former Treasury Secretary and president of Harvard, had called our tax plan "dishonest" and referred to me as stupid or a liar or both. Fareed repeated Larry's contention that our "plan is dishonest because it claims that what amounts to a $1,300 tax cut per worker, per household, somehow gets magically translated into $4,000 or more than that by the alchemy of your analysis."[10]

I replied to Fareed, first addressing the tone of Larry Summer's remarks, saying that if he thought we made an error, he should have described it in detail. But the ad hominem was "not becoming of a former Treasury secretary." I then called out Larry and other liberal economists savaging us in the media for making "horrendous Econ 101 blunders."[11]

Some critics delivered their objections respectfully. I had many conversations with Janet Yellen, President Biden's Treasury secretary, then chairman of the Federal Reserve Board and a former CEA chair. Her insights were valuable to me. She was very skeptical that our tax cuts would make a big difference in income. But she was always polite, criticizing my logic, not me personally.

But not Larry Summers. He wrote in the *Washington Post* that if you believe our tax reform plan would make a difference, then "you believe in tooth fairies and ludicrous supply-side economics."[12] When I pushed back on Larry's attacks, he doubled down, saying about my support for tax cuts, "I am proudly guilty of asserting that it is some combination of dishonest, incompetent and absurd."[13]

Other liberal economists, people I had considered colleagues and friends, added to the chorus.

During the campaign, the Tax Policy Center—a project of the liberal, partisan Urban Institute and Brookings Institution, both aligned with the Obama administration—produced a paper by five economists that pooh-poohed an early version of our tax plan. The paper asserted that our proposed cuts would cause tax receipts to plunge by $6.2 trillion in the first decade and explode the federal debt.

They conceded that our marginal tax rate cuts "would boost incentives to work, save, and invest if interest rates do not change."[14]

The Tax Policy Center followed up with a remarkably sloppy paper in September 2017, that agreed that the tax cuts would have a brief, sugar-high effect on wages. "However, because the plan causes budget deficits that would eventually reduce investment and the capital stock, it would ultimately depress both market wages and labor supply."[15]

The Tax Policy Center shook the liberal beehive, and as I frequently went on television as a spokesman, the bees were soon swarming to sting me.

Howard Gleckman of the Tax Policy Center tweeted that our projected wage increases derived from a reduction in corporate taxes "is based on some sloppy and highly controversial methodology."[16]

My predecessor as CEA chair and old friend Austan Goolsbee tweeted, "Why is Hassett saying this stuff?"[17]

Another CEA predecessor, Jason Furman, tweeted: "Poorly designed, temporary, deficit-financed tax cuts have been consistently shown to reduce growth which will lower wages not raise them."[18]

The dire projections of the Tax Policy Center were cited by Democrats who opposed our bill. They also spooked some Republicans, who took in the theory that reduced taxes would create a level of debt that would sink any benefit.

I worked closely with key members of Congress, especially Republicans like Congressman Kevin Brady, chairman of the House Ways and Means Committee, and Senator Orrin Hatch, chairman of the Senate Finance Committee, to keep them in sync with the White House. I worked with committee staff to fine-tune the brackets for the tax cuts at a fiscally responsible level. But many devils lurked in the details. Members of Congress pointed out that if our tax cuts were to pass by the end of December, businesses could expense all of their capital equipment immediately, rather than depreciating it over time. Anticipating this benefit, business could have well quit buying equipment altogether in the fourth quarter of 2017, causing a recession. We convinced Congress to announce when the tax cuts passed that expensing would be retroactive to October, thus eliminating the incentive to delay investment.

Along the way, there were many concessions and fine details added.

Senator Marco Rubio wanted a bigger child tax credit. Ivanka was excited by this proposal as well, so we doubled the credit to get his crucial vote.

Senator Bob Corker and a group of conservative deficit-hawks were worried that our tax cuts were going to blow up the deficit. He and many of his Republican peers were concerned that we would not generate positive economic effects big enough to justify the tax cuts. I replied that he was looking at projections as a static model and not scoring the dynamic, or feedback, effects. There is a virtuous cycle when new investment is created, one that generates new jobs which in turn generate more tax revenue. I explained how these benefits would grow over longer time frames. I also asked Senator Corker and other Republicans to consider the impact our insane corporate tax structure, which could not have been better designed to export U.S. jobs and business, would have on future economic growth, and the impact *that* would have on the federal deficit in the future.

The White House absolutely had to have Bob Corker on its side. We had to demonstrate to him that the country would be well served even if the lowest estimates of our projections came to pass. I went to the Hill often to play computer simulations for Senator Corker and a number of his Republican colleagues. Five months after my tense nomination hearing, the senator's personal skepticism of me was spilling over into our budget talks.

Senator Ron Johnson insisted on adding an additional tax break for small businesses that reduced their taxes as S corporations. Senator Johnson was adamant that we not be seen as favoring bigger businesses that registered with the IRS as C corporations. I was dispatched to Johnson's Senate office to negotiate on behalf of the White House. I explained to the senator that no change was really needed since it would be easy and cheap for S corporations to change their registration in response to the new law.

"Kevin, you're thinking like an economist not a politician," he replied.

What mattered most, he explained, was signaling to his small business constituency that their concerns were being looked after. I saw his point, which was not just political. The wrong impression could have an impact on economic confidence. We needed Senator Johnson's vote and made the late change. Then Senator Johnson came back with a list of changes for the taxes of small businesses that he demanded if we were to win his support.

The president was not interested in such minutiae.

"I'm not gonna list the five million things I want," the president said repeatedly. He then set down his two non-negotiables: corporate tax cuts and a big tax cut for the American middle class. He wanted his own tax staff and the committee staffs to do the best they could with the details required for the bill to pass.

As we struggled to get a solid basis of support on Capitol Hill, I came to fully appreciate the damage the Tax Policy Center was causing with its continuous stream of negative reviews of our tax policies. Chuck Schumer spoke for the monolithic Democratic opposition when he said of our plan, "The more it's in the sun, the more it stinks."[19] The *Financial Times* declared it "built for plutocrats."[20] Thirteen House Republicans, mostly from dark blue California, New Jersey, and New York, whose constituents would lose part of the federal subsidy for their state taxes, came out in opposition to the bill.[21]

The tax cuts seemed about dead, killed by all of the negative press. When the prospects for passing the bill were at their lowest, John Kelly presided over a despondent senior staff meeting in the Roosevelt Room with Gary, Jared, and Ivanka in attendance, as well as Sarah Huckabee Sanders, still fairly new as White House press secretary.

Marc Short, legislative director briefed us: "We can't really pass tax cuts because the moderate Republican senators are really upset. The Tax Policy Center report is all over the media. And Republicans are especially upset that the White House hasn't done anything to rebut it. They need cover if they are going to support us."

"It feels like the tax cuts are dead because the Tax Policy Center killed it," Kelly said. "Like they seem to kill every tax bill ever."

I didn't like what I was hearing. If the opposition was beating us through a poorly reasoned white paper, then I must not have been doing my job right. It was my fault. But I knew that I could get the bill back on track with a change of approach.

"No, the tax cuts are not dead," I said. "I'm going to go to the Tax Policy Center. And I'm going to give a talk, take their questions, and address their report." I added some Marine-like flourishes to the last part. I was genuinely angry that they were publishing such partisan, tendentious material that, in my view, harmed ordinary Americans. But I probably went too far to try to sound like a Marine, something I could never be.

Still, General Kelly smiled as if one of his Marines had just promised to take out a machine gun nest.

I contacted the Tax Policy Center (TPC), who courteously agreed to let me have my say. I often wing my remarks, but given the importance of this event, I labored over my lecture, which covered the main points in our rebuttal. I showed it to Gary.

"I like what you've got here, and it does indeed kick their asses," he said. "But the only people who will understand that this kicks their ass will be other economists as nerdy as you. Let me fiddle with it a bit."

So Gary recast my speech, adding in more accessible language and making the ideas clearer and more intuitive for non-economists.

With my draft ready, on October 5, 2017, I found myself facing a hundred TPC fellows and staff at a lectern at the Urban Institute.

"Taxes matter," I told them. "They impact the economy. It is scientifically indefensible to say—as the TPC report of last Friday does—that 'the framework [would] have little macroeconomic feedback effect.' It is simply inconsistent, with mountains of evidence that I am about to discuss, to have 'no' growth effects from tax changes this significant. It's inaccurate.

"I am sure many people in these halls have been struck and perhaps even dismayed by the pushback from around Washington regarding the TPC report," I said. "That's what happens when you behave irresponsibly.

"This plan is pro-growth. On the individual side it is pro-work. When you get more of an economic input like work, you get more economic output—and you get more economic growth. And on the corporate side, companies will no longer be incentivized to offshore, and what they save in taxes should help raise corporate investment and wages . . ."

I then turned to the political effect of their misinformation campaign.

"I think we can all agree that the TPC report did not, to say the least, contribute to the mood of bipartisan cooperation that has been so common in past successful attempts to reform the tax code. First, there are many parts of the plan that are still to be determined, yet the TPC report chose to make assumptions and publish an analysis that is unlikely to have much to do with the final bill. To the extent that such imagined numbers are used to attack the process would hardly be considered a constructive contribution."

After taking them to task for making up parts of the bill that had not yet been agreed to, I criticized the group for moving the goalposts on statically scored revenue costs.

"I frankly just don't understand what the purpose of a document is that shows a score for one number when there is agreement that the bill has to score to something else."

Columnist George Will, no admirer of Donald Trump and no friend of his administration, observed:

> Speaking recently to the Tax Policy Center and the Tax
> Foundation—left- and right-leaning, respectively—Hassett
> defended the administration's tax plan, although important
> provisions remain undecided. He criticized the TPC for a
> premature analysis that used "imagined numbers" to antici-
> pate the consequences of a bill still being written. And he

said that while the plan allows for a $1.5 trillion revenue loss in a decade "statically scored" (i.e., not allowing for the plan's stimulative effects), the TPC analysis "ignored any growth effects from tax reform and suggested there would be none," and "makes assumptions that would deliver" a $2.4 trillion revenue loss. He questioned the TPC scoring for this number "when there is agreement that the bill has to score" $1.5 trillion.[22]

Larry Kudlow, who would later replace Gary Cohn as head of the NEC, opined on CNBC that I had "spanked" the TPC and taken it to "the woodshed" in public. "Perhaps his toughest criticism of all, Hassett called the Tax Policy Center findings 'scientifically indefensible,'" he wrote.[23]

To this day, it saddens me that it came to that. But as we went on the offense, we fell back into an effective sync as a team, from the president to his econ team, all supporting a media campaign. Our assertive stance had an effect. In late November, 137 prominent economists signed an open letter supporting our plan. We began to get warmer responses from potential fence-sitters among Republicans in Congress, whose staff began to shower us with detailed questions. I enjoyed strong technical support all along the way from what Will called "America's best economic 'faculty.'" To name only two, among our standouts were Richard Burkhauser, professor emeritus from Cornell, who made many great contributions, and Steve Braun, CEA director of Macroeconomic Forecasting.

Like a balloon just barely scraping over the Matterhorn, our tax law passed on reconciliation in the Senate by a vote of 51–48, on December 20, 2017. President Trump signed it into law on December 22.

No sooner did the bill pass than the liberal intelligentsia swung into gear to portray it as a disaster with lies and misleading statistics. One effect of the bill was to encourage companies to take advantage of the 35 percent rates on expensing capital equipment in December, before it was reduced to 21 percent. There was a brief moment when firms could deduct capital purchases such as a new machine from their taxes against the higher corporate tax rate that was in place until the end of 2017. Spend a dollar in December, and you get a 35-cent break from the government. Spend the same dollar in January, and you only get 21 cents. So the bill created a boom in investment that in actuality happened before the lower tax rates were technically in effect.

Instead of describing this growth, critics pointed to weak growth in capital equipment in January, neglecting the capital spending boom that happened in December thanks to the tax-law change. Spending went to a higher level and grew even higher from there, albeit at a slower rate of growth. In my media appearances and discussions with top economists, I pointed out that the January figures showed growth on top of what was already a very high level of capital expenditure. If anything, the capital spending increases we saw were a testament to the strength of the design of the tax cuts.

While the Democrats doubled down on their disaster talk, I made a public bet with Austan Goolsbee, President Obama's CEA chair, on a panel at the American Economic Association that income inequality would decrease and that African Americans, whose prospects had stagnated under Obama, would be prime beneficiaries of the economy shaped by Trump's tax cuts.

Once the tax cuts were passed and Americans could see the benefits of the reforms for themselves, the attacks began to take on a desperate quality. The economic mood of the country was clearly shifting.

Walmart, the largest private employer in the United States, announced on January 11, 2018, that it was raising its starting wage from $9 to $11, expanding maternity and parental leave benefits, introducing new financial assistance for employees looking to adopt, and providing a onetime cash bonus for eligible employees of up to $1,000.[24] Apple, then the largest publicly listed company in the world by stock market capitalization announced employee bonuses of $2,500 worth of restricted stock units in response to the Tax Cuts and Jobs Act. The company also announced that it would be incurring a $38 billion tax bill in order to repatriate $245 billion in offshore cash.[25] JPMorgan Chase announced a $20 billion investment program to open 400 new branches and add 3,000 jobs. The bank also announced that it would be raising hourly wages for 22,000 full- and part-time U.S. employees.[26] Good news was coming in droves. And even if liberal journalists didn't want to cover it, Americans could see the benefits of the new situation for themselves.

★ ★ ★

Two years later, Gary and I were both back in the private sector. We took to the editorial pages of the *Wall Street Journal* to review the impact the tax law had had on the economy and on the American people. So many elite economists and liberal media had predicted a disaster. Where was it?

We noted that we had argued that tax cuts, by making it cheaper to install new plants and machinery, would increase the amount of capital per worker, driving up productivity, which drives up wages. We had made the controversial, and much ridiculed, prediction that our plan would increase family incomes by $4,000 in three to five years, with blue-collar workers benefiting disproportionately.

As it turned out, we were proven wrong. For wages, the numbers were even better than we had expected. Quoting directly from the piece:

> This predicted increase in capital has materialized. . . . Capital spending was 4.5 percent higher in 2018 than pre-TCJA [Tax Cuts and Jobs Act] blue-chip forecasts, and the trend continued in 2019. The extra capital improved productivity and wages and, as expected, did so especially for those in lower-paying jobs. The numbers are striking. Over the past year, nominal wages for the lowest 10 percent of American workers jumped 7 percent. The growth rate for those without a high school diploma was 9 percent. . . . And about that $4,000? Real disposable personal income per household has increased $6,000 since the tax cuts were passed.[27]

So it didn't take three to five years to see big changes in family incomes. And they hadn't risen by $4,000. They actually shot up by $6,200 a year. That was a real difference in people's lives. Right before the coronavirus shut down the economy, Americans had felt an $8,000 increase in yearly income.

The results simply go on and on. Almost 7 million Americans were lifted off food stamps since the election as food insecurity fell. Three million fewer people were enrolled in Medicaid and the Children's Health Insurance Program. The total number of veterans reported experiencing homelessness in 2018 decreased 5.4 percent, falling to nearly half the number reported in 2010.

Over 1.4 million people were lifted out of poverty since 2017, and nearly 2.5 million people have been lifted out of poverty since 2016. We wrote:

"Those who say that the strong economy under President Trump is merely a continuation of past trends are in full-scale denial.

"Before Mr. Trump took office in January 2017, the Congressional Budget Office forecast the creation of only two million jobs by this point. The economy has in fact created seven million jobs since January 2017."[28]

Our Opportunity Zones spurred $75 billion in new investments by the end of 2019.[29] The poverty rate for African Americans reached a record low in 2018.[30] President Trump saw many economic reports that were worth celebrating during my time in the White House, but these facts were the ones that filled him with the most joy.

* * *

While the Tax Cuts and Jobs Act began to liberate Americans to invest and work again, I got pulled into a public struggle between the president and Jerome Powell, whom he had chosen in early 2018 to replace Janet Yellen as chairman of the Federal Reserve Board. For weeks it seemed as if Yellen might stay. I encountered her in the hallway of the

West Wing twice, and both times we both implicitly felt that she was likely to be reappointed.

But President Trump chose Jerome Powell, "Jay" to his friends, on the strength of Steven Mnuchin's endorsement.

In the fall of 2018, Powell, seeing the revival of the economy, began to pull away from the near zero interest rates that the Fed had adopted in response to the economic meltdown that had occurred a decade before. Powell saw this as a prudent measure to manage the monetary supply and perhaps offset the risk of inflation. President Trump saw the rate hikes as hamstringing his economic recovery.

"So far, I'm not even a little bit happy with my selection of Jay," President Trump told the *Washington Post*. "Not even a little bit . . . the Fed is way off-base with what they're doing."[31] The president believed that Powell's two rate hikes were shaving as much as a half-a-point off of economic growth, endangering the economy that was going to be Trump's prime bragging point for the 2020 election.

In August 2018, the president tweeted: "My only question is, who is our bigger enemy, Jay Powell or Chairman Xi?"[32]

By fall, speculation that Trump would fire Powell was widespread.

I believed the president had a point. The rate increases were coming too early, too quick, and could endanger the recovery. And it was galling that the supposedly independent Federal Reserve waited for a Republican to be president to raise interest rates. Still, the optics were awful. This episode had all the hallmarks of the worst tendencies of the Trump presidency. Donald Trump would choose someone—a cursory list includes Jeff Sessions, John Kelly, Jim Mattis, Rex Tillerson, Bill Barr, and ultimately, his own vice president, Mike Pence—only to turn on them in a very public way. Never before had a president made such a sport out of attacking his own Cabinet and appointees.

Worse, firing Powell would have savaged the reputation of the Federal Reserve Board as an objective and independent manager of the nation's money supply. The credibility of the dollar would have been compromised. The stock market might have crashed, doing far more damage to the economy than Powell's rate hikes.

Just the perception that Powell could be fired had already hurt confidence. The market had its worst year in a decade in 2018, with the S&P falling more than 6 percent. In fact, in December it had its biggest percentage decline since the Great Depression.[33]

But along with some legal minds in the West Wing, the White House counsel's office and I had been doing some research. We found that it may not have been possible for the president to fire Powell and told him in the Oval Office. We could maybe fire him as chairman, but he would be able to stay on as a member of the board. The other members could decide to treat him as chairman, and that would be as far as matters could go.

That discussion stayed private, but at one memorable press conference in December 2018, I took the opportunity to respond to a reporter's question by announcing that Powell's job was "100 percent" safe. I didn't ask permission to do that. I did it because I believe in transparency, and I believed the issue was resolved, and what I said was true. I did not know whether President Trump would be angry that I said so, but I also knew that he understood that as CEA chair I would always just say what I believed to be true, not recite politically calculated talking points.

The markets rebounded and resumed an upward climb and had one of the biggest days on record. And I very quickly found out that, perhaps because of the market response, the president approved. He was flying back from overseas on Air Force One, and he called me up and said, "You just caused the biggest jump in markets ever. Great job!"

Behind the scenes, I continued the practice of having lunch with the Fed chairman, taking in his views and sharing them with the president, and sharing the president's views and adding in a few of my own. In the end, Powell eased off the rate hikes and kept his job, the stock market calmed down, the recovery deepened without inflation, and the president relaxed.

There was one unfortunate consequence of the spat. Steven Mnuchin was one of the most insightful advisors President Trump had. Because he had proposed Powell for the Fed job, Mnuchin had to absorb abuse from the president at the start of virtually every meeting for his recommendation from that point on. I will always remember how graceful Mnuchin was under attack, even when the president's attacks were viciously seconded by Mnuchin's foe Peter Navarro.

★ ★ ★

The deep impact the coronavirus has had on the lives of millions of Americans makes it hard to remember how significant and robust the results of the tax cuts were on people's lives. As it turned out, I believe we created a strong underlying economy that set a foundation for an easier recovery.

We know what works. We constructed a theory of what would happen if taxes were cut, and then the theory was tested by data. Our predictions were accurate down to the decimal point, and our critics were proven wrong. As the policies of the Biden administration are implemented and supported by the same individuals who said the Trump plan couldn't work, we will surely have a fresh opportunity to see what failure looks like.

What is good news for people is bad news for socialism—higher wages for those at the bottom, plummeting poverty, capital flowing into what previously were no-man's lands to create businesses and jobs and hope—such results are a serious challenge to socialists seeking power. This economic experiment's success was a mortal threat to the Drift and had to be stopped at all costs. I thought things were ugly in Washington when I started. But the success of our policies, instead of winning converts, raised the level of political conflict to unbelievable heights. The sweep of history has a mighty counterpunch.

## CHAPTER SEVEN

# Five Million Hours and Counting

U nder socialism, politicians—not consumers—pick industrial winners and losers. The more I saw of how business is conducted in Washington and how government thumbs the scales, the more I saw how special insider deals are accelerating America's Drift toward socialism. Perhaps the best example of my ringside view of the Drift came when a meeting was called to discuss a law called the Jones Act that regulates U.S. shipping. In a truly socialist world, shipping in America would look very much like it already does. Our attempts to stop the Drift, and our failure to do so, provide important lessons about the power of the ruling elite and the difficulty involved in unseating them.

I couldn't help but occasionally glance over the president's shoulder at the window facing the Washington Monument and the National Mall. Even through green-tinted bullet-proof glass, I could see it was one of those fine cherry-blossom spring days in Washington that makes it feel like a crime to be indoors.

"This Jones Act, it doesn't make any sense," the president said. "We should see if we can come up with some fixes. I hope we can do that."

He scanned the room, looking for approval.

Nods came from Larry Kudlow, who had replaced Gary Cohn as National Economic Council director a year before, as well as from me. Peter Navarro, who had rebounded from his demotion, looked back at the president, stone-faced. I knew that Larry and I had all the facts on our side, but Peter and others in the administration had something else: raw political power. It was not just them. There is a giant industry in Washington, D.C., dedicated to protecting profoundly stupid regulation. When considering the forces arrayed against him, the deregulatory accomplishments of President Trump seem all the more remarkable.

The Jones Act is a 101-year-old law that requires any shipments between American ports be carried by ships built, owned, and operated by American citizens or permanent residents. This law was passed in the aftermath of World War I, with the intention of strengthening American shipbuilding. It has long since become a case study in how severe unintended consequences can be.

As my deputy and colleague Casey Mulligan notes in his White House memoir, *You're Hired!*, at CEA we worked to show that by increasing costs by a factor of five to eight, "the law has by now all but ended domestic coastal shipping and U.S. ship building."[1] When countries that had laws similar to the Jones Act dropped them decades before, they doubled their coastwise cargo carriage. Meanwhile America's fleet spun into decline.[2] In 1950, the United States had 400 ocean-going ships compliant with the Jones Act. By 2015, the United States had fewer than 100. Annual tonnage carried by these ships fell from 250 million in 1980 to 70 million in 2016.[3] Drive around Europe, and marvel at how many container ships you see in every port. In the United States, there are practically none. It's what happens when government controls the means of production. This has a huge cost to the United States because shipping is a much more efficient way to move products. Floating requires no energy, and boats don't make potholes.

Worse, the Jones Act acts as a tax on Hawaii, Alaska, and Puerto Rico, the last of which pays almost $400 per resident in costs added by high Jones Act rates.[4] Economic consultant John Dunham reported in

2019 that "the Jones Act is a contributor to the poor economic situation in the Commonwealth of Puerto Rico."[5] And in Hawaii, a large ranch on the Big Island, unable to afford Jones Act rates, is forced to charter a 747 every week to fly their cattle to the mainland.[6] (Talk about steerage!)

Material that could be transported most efficiently by ship—across the Great Lakes, for example—is sent by truck because Jones Act shipping is too expensive. The Jones Act thus adds to congestion on the nation's highways, which is bad for road safety and the environment. Ships produce 10 to 40 grams of carbon dioxide per kilometer, trucks 60 to 150 grams for the same weight and distance.[7] Millions of tons of ammonia, sulfur, nonferrous scrap, and nonferrous ore that go by ship between U.S. ports must first be exported to Canada to be legal.

The most absurd drawback to the Jones Act is its shipping of American-produced natural gas, cooled to its liquid state for transport. In the last decade, the United States has reemerged as an energy powerhouse, becoming the world's number one producer of natural gas. The replacement of coal in electricity production by natural gas has put the United States in the forefront of reductions in carbon emissions (with or without the Paris Agreement on climate change). In addition to about a dozen U.S. liquefied natural gas (LNG) terminals, ExxonMobil and the nation of Qatar are building an enormous terminal on the Gulf Coast of East Texas, capable of shipping 2.1 billion cubic feet of natural gas a day to the world. One billion feet a day is enough to power 5 million U.S. homes.[8]

But none of this LNG will go straight to U.S. households. Because of the Jones Act, shipping rates of oil originating from the U.S. Gulf Coast are three to five times greater than from Nigeria, Saudi Arabia, and Canada. In fact, it is cheaper to ship oil from the Gulf Coast to another country and then back to the East Coast than to ship it directly. Puerto Rico, despite being relatively close to Gulf Coast ports, has to import oil from foreign countries, including communist Venezuela.

On the East Coast, consumers must pay $9 per thousand cubic feet for natural gas from Russia. In *You're Hired!* Casey reports that our work found that:

the empty ships then make a short trip down the East Coast where they refill with LNG at bargain prices as low as $3 per thousand cubic feet and then cross the ocean again to deliver to their final customers in Pakistan. From the point of view of the consumers in Massachusetts and Pakistan, and from producers in Russia and the U.S., this transport system is hardly different from running illegal bootlegging routes up the American East Coast while delivering natural gas directly from Russia to Pakistan. Either way, the Russians get to pocket $6 per thousand cubic feet ($9 in Massachusetts minus $3 in Maryland or Georgia) at America's expense. . . . You're welcome, Gazprom! You're welcome, international shippers![9]

Larry and I explained all of this to the president, who shook his head in disgust. If Donald Trump loathed anything, it is stupid inefficiencies like these. Above all, he despised what deals like this reveal about the squalid, rent-seeking behavior of Washington's special interests and their lack of concern for the rest of the country. As a businessman, President Trump saw the hidden costs such sweetheart deals heap on working Americans. Larry and I did not, however, argue for a repeal of the Jones Act. Instead, we argued for a more modest goal: the president should approve a waiver for LNG. Given that the United States has no LNG carriers, such a waiver would not have displaced a single mariner job or ship.[10] My staff did a calculation that suggested that New Englanders had paid an extra $500 million to foreign gas companies during the latest cold spell because of the Jones Act.

But Jones Act supporters were undeterred. Peter did his histrionic best to portray the need to protect American shipping that largely does not exist. This set up Transportation Secretary Elaine Chao to make the cooler argument that before making a decision, the president should arrange a White House meeting with members of Congress. Unstated was the fact that Elaine's family runs a shipping business which, while not a Jones Act company, could profit from the absence of U.S.

competitors. And being married to the Senate majority leader perhaps moved the debate to terrain that was less hostile to the policy.

Shortly afterwards, the president met with the senators from Louisiana and Mississippi with the personable House Republican whip, Steve Scalise, front and center. The delegation, surprisingly, did not seem to understand that the issue at hand was a narrow one—a waiver for LNG. They came prepared to defend the Jones Act in its entirety. In a sense, this was the right strategy for them. An LNG waiver would demonstrate to the world just how costly and nonsensical the Jones Act is. If New England has to pay $500 million extra for natural gas in a cold winter month, it's a small price to pay to keep the Jones Act lobby off your back.

A president has to pick and choose his battles. Though taken aback by their willingness to perpetuate such a broken system, Donald Trump decided that his political capital was best spent elsewhere. The Jones Act would have to wait for the president's second term. After a meeting about another matter with Jared and the president, the president looked at me and said, "You are right about the Jones Act, but the political lift is so large that we will have to come back to it later with a complete plan to undo it. I am not dropping it, I am postponing action. We have much more important things to do."

Elaine Chao, a short time later, was recognized by the American Maritime Partnership as a "Maritime Hero" alongside "World War Two Merchant Marines."

No other policy debate better illustrates the destructive power of the Swamp. The political constituency that still defends the Jones Act largely resides in Louisiana, another literal swamp. But at least the rent-seeking of special interests, like shippers protected by the Jones Act, makes sense. Senators and congressmen from Mississippi and Louisiana are protecting the jobs of mariners, ship builders, and dock workers in their states, even if they do so at the expense of the rest of the country. Water is the most efficient medium through which to transport things. If you take a rubber duck and push it in your bathtub, it keeps going. Yet the U.S. has essentially no water transport between U.S. ports because of the Jones Act.

This is great for the Jones Act companies and great for the railroads that get all of that freight business instead of a healthy maritime fleet, but terrible for the economy.

Protecting the Jones Act, however, gets politicians reelected. And to be fair, it would be hard to imagine any member of Congress going to his or her home district, looking voters in the eye, and saying, "I am going to put you out of work, defund your schools, and destroy your community." Once a protectionist law like the Jones Act goes into operation, communities develop around the protected industry that make it political agony to even consider changing it.

Let's take a moment to sort out all of the costs of unnecessary regulation.

Increases in regulation decrease rates of new business entry, which is unfortunate because newer firms tend to make greater contributions to economy-wide productivity, which in turn means higher wages for Americans. Increased regulation may even explain much of America's recent productivity slowdown, which exacerbated the stagnation of wages under Bush and Obama.

Local regulations can cost the national economy. According to one estimate, for instance, the relaxation of restrictive land-use regulations in just the three cities of New York, San Jose, and San Francisco between 1964 and 2009 would have increased the 2009 U.S. economy by 8.9 percent, translating into an almost $9,000 bost in average wages for all American workers.[11] Such overregulation damages people's ability to relocate to where jobs exist. Geographic mobility in the United States has ebbed to an all-time low, as regulatory barriers, especially at the state and local levels, make living in high-priced cities unattainable for many Americans. But many of America's cities, where jobs are plentiful, are unavailable to Americans because the local regulation burden on land-use and construction have made houses unaffordable.

No state has done a better job at killing jobs than California. One example: Beauty and personal care have long been an important first rung of a ladder that has led many people with modest educational credentials to rise in those professions, sometimes even to ownership of their own shops. But one must have cosmic patience to pursue these professions in the Golden State.

California's Board of Barbering and Cosmetology requires 1,600 hours of education and hands-on training before taking a licensing test for cosmetology. An additional 3,200 hours of apprenticeship and 220 hours of related training are required for licensing. Not to be outdone, Oregon requires 1,450 hours of education and training for hair design licensing and 350 hours for nail technology, along with 150 hours of safety or infection control training and 100 hours of career development at a state-licensed career school.[12]

In the 1950s, less than 5 percent of the workforce was licensed, compared with about 18 percent in the 1980s. By 2000, this had grown to at least 20 percent; and in 2003, more than 800 occupations required licensing in at least one state. In 2008, 35 percent of employees across the United States were either licensed or certified by the government, with 29 percent licensed.[13]

It is easy to see why national and local politicians act in ways that benefit large or powerful home district constituencies. Harder to understand is the largely unseen destruction of American jobs and income caused by a permanent Washington bureaucracy that specializes in red tape and rulemaking that serves no constituency, except perhaps by generating work for attorneys. These rules cost the nation dearly but often do nothing to serve the economy, the well-being of the American people, or the environment. They are simply imposed by the bureaucrats to serve their internal processes, which in turn validate their . . . power? Sense of self-worth? Justification for their jobs?

The costs of local regulations are onerous. At the national level, the costs of regulation are obscene. How much? For a start, reports estimate as much as $2 trillion in compliance costs.[14] According to the Office of Management and Budget, Americans spent 9.8 billion hours devoted to compliance paperwork in a recent year. Imagine if those almost 10 billion hours were used by American workers to create output equal to average hourly earnings. It would pump $245 billion into the wallets of American families.

Every modern president has grappled with this problem of overregulation. Every president has failed, but Trump fought the hardest and accomplished the most.

Under President Jimmy Carter, the Paperwork Reduction Act of 1980 was designed to reduce the total paperwork burden that the federal government imposes on private businesses. What did Washington do with that mandate? The paperwork burden for regulatory compliance went from 7 billion hours in 1997 to 9.8 billion hours in 2009—an average annual increase of 2.8 percent. (Someday, perhaps, we should compute these paperwork costs in terms of forests as well as man-hours.)

No one disputes the need for clean air. In recent decades, the United States has made enormous strides in clearing our air of smog. For anyone who spent time in Pasadena, California, in the previous century, it is a joy to go to Pasadena today and see the San Gabriel Mountains. But the Clean Air Act, which made much of this possible (along with the ever-increasing energy efficiency of American business) reached a trade-off in which the costs of regulation exceed any environmental benefit. The act's stricter air quality regulations are associated with an almost 2.6 percent decline in productivity in manufacturing plants. The Clean Air Act may have decreased productivity by an estimated 4.8 percent, roughly $21 billion (in 2010 dollars) annually, or about 8.8 percent of the manufacturing sector's profits during the relevant period.

Those are costs that can be measured in terms of jobs, income, and family well-being. And yet, whenever an administration questions these costs or seeks to tweak them to the benefit of working Americans, the permanent bureaucracy reacts with feigned alarm and a compliant media broadcasts hysterical claims, with headlines such as "Administration Guts Clear Air Act!" The media, with their mindless and reflexive defense of wasteful regulation, advances our Drift toward socialism. The mechanism that can defend even the insane Jones Act is a historical, formidable opponent.

Because of the hysterical reaction of the media to modest adjustments to regulations, there were only slight differences of degree between recent Republican and Democratic administrations on regulation—until Donald Trump. From 2000 to 2016, the federal government put out an average of over 100 more significant final regulations than the number our administration finalized in 2019. And many of the rules the Trump administration published were deregulatory actions that did not impose burdens on Americans but lifted them.

The Federal Register page count is one rule-of-thumb measure of an administration's record on regulation. When George W. Bush became president, there were 64,438 pages in the register. When he left office, there were almost 80,000 pages. Not to be outdone, President Obama hit 95,894 pages in his last year in office.[15]

Under Obama, federal regulations grew by an unprecedented 8 percent per year, tying an anchor around the necks of small businesses struggling to learn how to comply with successive regulations. CEA determined that in just the first six months of the Trump administration, businesses spent 5 million fewer working hours coping with regulations—time that could be applied to productive work.

Another measure of an administration's real record on regulation includes the number of times restrictive terms like "shall" or "required" are used. Under President Obama, the number of restrictive terms increased by about 120,000. For President George W. Bush, the increase was about 105,000. Under President Trump, such regulatory restrictions actually decreased.[16] The libertarian Cato Institute reports that the total number of economically significant regulations issued under Trump was less than 50 percent of those issued by Bush and Obama.[17]

Despite the successes of our administration, before Joe Biden came to office, the regulatory state was still imposing $1.9 *trillion* in costs according to the Competitive Enterprise Institute.[18] Some part of that cost is necessary to protect the environment, the economy, and human health. But much of it is still sheer waste. That waste constitutes an enormous hidden tax on families. In fact, if our regulatory state were a country, it would be bigger than Canada's entire economy. The idea that we are getting more than $1.9 trillion in health and safety benefits from these rules is laughable.

If one-half of that amount could be reinvested in American industry and jobs, think of what that would mean for the family income, stability, and prosperity of Americans. Instead, we tolerate this extraordinary degree of waste, year after year, because it is unseen. The most remarkable aspect of this is that aside from the bureaucracy and lawyers, there really isn't a constituency for these regulations and this waste. Yet politicians in the Swamp double down on overregulation, year after year.

One of Donald Trump's favorite tropes was to talk about how "stupid" American leadership is compared to that of other countries. When it comes to overregulation, that's certainly true. According to OECD reporting, the United States tends to be more regulated than its OECD peers. In fact, the OECD's calculations place the United States twenty-seventh out of thirty-five countries in terms of regulation, behind France, Chile, and the Czech Republic.[19] In other words, there is a Jones Act under every rock, and a viper waiting to protect it.

Other countries are indeed often quicker to recognize the costs of doing business than we are. Both Canada and the United Kingdom have implemented similar processes for administrative rulemaking. In 2012, Canada enacted a "One-for-One" for regulatory requirement, while the United Kingdom imposed a "One-In, One-Out" rule in 2011, meaning that for every new rule, an old one must be thrown out. In the UK, for example, the government has reduced business burdens by an estimated £963 million. This effort has been so successful that the government changed the rule to "One-In, Three-Out" through 2020.[20]

★ ★ ★

As soon as he became president, Donald Trump took aim at red tape and regulation like a heat-seeking missile. In 2017, President Trump issued four executive orders directing agencies to review current regulations. The first, Executive Order 13771, instructed agencies to repeal two regulations for every new regulation and to ensure that the total incremental cost of all new regulations does not exceed zero. Another executive order, Executive Order 13772, provided core principles for regulating the U.S. financial system in ways that emphasized empowering individuals to make informed, independent financial decisions. Another, Executive Order 13777, required agencies to review all existing regulations in order to highlight excessive regulation, which includes analysis to identify regulations that are outdated, that eliminate jobs or inhibit job creation, or have costs that exceed their benefits.[21] And finally, Executive Order 13783 focused on energy regulations, requiring agencies to review existing regulations that may burden the development of domestically produced energy resources. These orders set up our administration to identify the low-hanging fruit in deregulation that yield big savings.

In the first autumn of the administration, we reported that agencies withdrew 635 proposed actions from the last year of the Obama administration. Agencies also reclassified another 944 active actions, with 700 put on hold and another 244 made inactive while placed under review. All these actions reflected Donald Trump's commitment to meaningful consideration and reconsideration of regulations. Of the new proposed rules and rules already under review, the administration published only 89 final rules, about 42 percent of the average number of final rules published annually during the past 10 years.[22]

In the Department of the Interior, we finalized 28 deregulatory actions, leading to a $1 billion cut in costs for business and jobs. The department's Bureau of Land Management proposed repealing rules regulating hydraulic fracturing that duplicate state regulatory efforts. The Department of Labor created plans to streamline its approval process for apprenticeship programs to help workers looking to participate in such programs. The Department of Transportation planned to issue a rule that would give passenger railroads increased flexibility in designing trains, including easing the regulatory burden for high-speed rail operation, which would increase competition in the passenger train market.

In that first executive order on regulation, President Trump, perhaps looking to the success of the British effort, instructed administrative agencies to consider whether earlier regulations are unnecessary before creating new ones. For example, the Department of Housing and Urban Development announced a top-to-bottom review of its manufactured housing rules to evaluate whether the compliance costs of these rules are justified given the shortage of affordable housing. By requiring the removal of two regulatory actions to offset the implementation of each new regulatory action, the "two-for-one rule" limited future regulatory costs. In this way, agencies ensured an overall outcome of zero net costs, or even cost savings.

Nowhere did regulatory reductions prove more beneficial than in the Environmental Protection Agency (EPA), which issues rules that often have impacts across the economy. President Trump's EPA administrator, Andrew Wheeler, issued a memo to bring transparency to the way the EPA implemented cost-benefit analysis, so the public and Congress could weigh each regulation fairly.

Previous administrations had attempted this, but with a subjective, watered-down metric. President Obama, for example, included escape hatches for the bureaucracy that contained nebulous standards like "equity," "fairness," and "human dignity."[23] Politicians and the public can weigh such values themselves. What voters and the people they elect needed was a transparent way to see the actual costs being spun out of the maze of government.

During the Obama years, I could see the stream of regulations flowing out of the West Wing from my perch at AEI a few blocks away. The Obama administration's regulatory abuses were affronts to the laws not only of economics but also of the United States. For instance, if you think President Trump overreacted in his attacks on "globalism," read the Obama administration's cost-benefit analysis of an environmental regulation of greenhouse gases, arguing that the global benefits outweighed the U.S. costs! That was the first time a U.S. regulation was, to my knowledge, justified on the basis of global benefits, in violation of American law.

The EPA was often the worst regulatory offender. Under Donald Trump, the EPA set out to cite the highest standard of scientific evidence in its cost-benefit reports. In enacting this rule, the EPA conducted "retrospective reviews" so it could look back on old regulations to examine whether projected benefits and costs were accurate. Had previous projections on a given rule been inflated or undervalued? Have regulations accumulated in a way that harms economic growth?[24] If so, we had a guide to help us on what to do next.

In the first eight months, the Trump administration issued 67 deregulatory actions and 3 regulatory actions, far outpacing the goal of 2 deregulatory actions for every 1 regulatory action.[25] That translated to more than $8.1 billion in present-value cost savings. Once fully in effect, 20 major deregulatory actions undertaken by the administration were calculated to save American consumers and businesses over $220 billion a year. Under President Trump's administration, regulatory costs tracked by the Office of Information and Regulatory Affairs fell by $50 billion, and costs were on track to fall by at least $52 billion in 2020. Nor were these giveaways to the rich. Deregulation in two key sectors—prescription drugs and internet access—helped the poorest fifth of households 8 times more than the richest fifth.[26]

I was able to report to the president that in just the first 6 months of his administration, businesses spent 5 million fewer working hours coping with regulations. Over 4 years, our deregulatory measures could save American households an average of $3,100 a year.

These were impressive numbers, the most impressive deregulatory impact from any administration ever. And yet, in that one presidential term, we had hardly made a dent.

★ ★ ★

In my time in the administration, my favorite example (among many) of the power of deregulation to help people actually comes, as odd as it sounds, from the manufacture of helicopter windshields. One of the most interesting things about working in the White House is that you are always close to people engaged in fascinating projects. For example, there were Navy SEALs on our floor who worked on secret missions which we never learned about. They loved to stop by the CEA at cocktail hour, and let's just say that one SEAL can outdrink a very large collection of economists. There was also a Coast Guard representative on our hall, and he knew everything about helicopters.

One afternoon the Coast Guard representative told me a story about a deregulatory effort he had helped with. Every helicopter needs a certain type of curved glass windshield. To test the windshield's night visibility, the Federal Aviation Administration (FAA) requires that a professional test pilot take the chopper for a ride. The FAA's intent was obviously good. But this regulation added $40,000 for each helicopter produced. The Trump administration, he told me, changed that rule so that an equally effective but vastly cheaper test in the factory could achieve the same goal. Instead of a dangerous flight, our deregulators suggested, perhaps it was smarter just to turn the lights out and test visibility when the helicopter got to the end of the production line.

That is not only money saved for Bell, Boeing, and Sikorsky. It is money that can be invested by those companies into being more productive, creating the potential for more jobs and better take-home pay for the people who work on the factory floor.

\* \* \*

I don't expect the Biden administration to appreciate stories that show how deregulatory efforts can help American families and businesses. Give Joe Biden his due; he's true to his word. For example, during the campaign, Biden promised: "I have been a consistent and strong advocate for the Jones Act and its mandate that only U.S.-flag vessels carry cargo in the coastwise trade."[27] If you live in Boston, expect to continue to pay through the nose for high-priced Russian energy.

In his first days in office, Joe Biden returned policy back to the nebulous, impossible-to-list feel-good categories that have no business in an economic measure. Those terms open the door to sophistries, as any harmful policy could now be justified as serving the climate or racial equality.

President Biden's early actions in office sent a clear message about the regulatory agenda soon to come. Within weeks of inauguration, Biden rescinded the permit for the Keystone XL Pipeline, throwing thousands out of work. While blue collar workers may have lost some high paying oil jobs, at least there will be some work in breaking the pipeline apart for scrap. And there will be plenty of work for U.S. diplomats as we repair the damage done to the economy of Canada, one of our closest allies and trading partners. But if you are a pipefitter or a welder, tough luck about losing years of steady work. And be sure to turn in all of your equipment before you leave.

While the media and Republicans fixated on Keystone, President Biden pulled a fast one, a measure barely noticed but with an impact a thousand times greater. President Biden issued one executive order with the narcotizing title, "Modernizing Regulatory Review."[28] It effectively ends the practice of subjecting every new regulation to a cost-benefit analysis, a practice in place since at least the Clinton administration. Regulators now do not even have to attempt to cook up numbers that justify their actions. The Drift has shifted to fast forward.

Biden made the change to transform the rule into "a tool to affirmatively promote regulations" and "to ensure swift and effective federal action" on the pandemic, the economy, racial inequality, and the "undeniable reality and accelerating threat of climate change."[29] By inserting values and concerns that cannot be quantified, the president essentially eliminated the ability of cost-benefit analysis to yield anything useful. Regulators could issue rules without first ensuring that those rules wouldn't have adverse economic effects. The bureaucrats were given free rein.

The left-wing HuffPost reported the memo was a break with "forty years of conservative policy."[30] If by "conservative" you mean "rational," then it most certainly is. HuffPost called Biden's order "game changing," saying "the memo could unleash a wave of stronger regulations to reduce income inequality, fight climate change, and protect public health. Among left-leaning experts on regulation, it's a signal that Biden could break with 40 years of conservative policy."

James Goodwin of the Center for Progressive Reform was even more rhapsodic: "I realize what I'm about to say to you sounds absurd. It has the potential to be the most significant action Biden took on day one."[31]

The liberals of yesteryear, from John F. Kennedy to Jimmy Carter, understood that excessive regulation creates costs that drain money away from jobs, from family income, from the tax base for schools, and from the healthcare system. They understood that excessive regulation hurts people, even if it is largely unseen. The Democratic Party of today, swept along by the Drift, sees executive orders and legislation as a means to express empathy and showcase politically correct concern. It is regulation as political wallpaper. The rational calculation of burdens heaped on working people and the families they support is not even a consideration.

Gone, too, is the sensible requirement that every new regulation be offset by the revocation of two more rules. The Trump administration far exceeded that self-set goal, getting rid of more than four rules for every new one implemented.[32] The Biden administration has no similar ambition. Expect the Federal Register under President Biden to exceed 100,000 pages. Somewhere, a forest is crying.

Trump's deregulatory agenda unwound decades of crazy and costly regulations. At CEA we did a deep dive to estimate how much all of this effort delivered to the American people. The report bore the profoundly sexy title, "The Economic Effects of Federal Deregulation since January 2017." In it, a team led by Casey Mulligan carefully estimated the economic benefit of the 20 largest deregulatory actions taken by the Trump administration. The study was steeped in data and math but had a simple conclusion. Trump's efforts had reduced the regulatory burden for

Americans by $220 billion per year, saving each American household $3,100 per year. The savings came because when businesses waste less money on silly regulations, they can lower their prices for consumers. We showed that this was exactly what happened.

Deregulation is perhaps the best example of the kind of benefits a disruptor like President Trump can have. And if he had won a second term to take on more burdensome regulations such as the Jones Act, the savings for Americans might have been twice as big. Looking back, it seems that our team did not fully understand the sweeping historical forces that we were fighting against, and thus came to a gun fight with a knife. Trump came in with a team of outsiders. When he left, he had a team that understood the machine that he had been up against. If a similar team ever does acquire power again, I would expect the Jones Act to go on the first day, as a demonstration to the rest of the deep state that the game is up.

## CHAPTER EIGHT

# What Makes a Country
# a Country

I came into the White House with fully formed ideas about national economic policy. But Donald Trump is nothing if not a disruptor who makes people take a second and third look at their closely held opinions. His passionate rhetoric forced me to reconsider a question I probably last thought of as a child: What makes America a country?

Is it all the wonderful geographic elements in *America the Beautiful*?—Nebraska's amber waves of grain, Colorado's purple mountain majesties?

Is it all the land and its features defined by its four borders with Canada, Mexico, and the Atlantic and Pacific Oceans?

Is it an ideal, the first country to be founded not on the concept of a kingdom or a tribe, but on the Enlightenment ideal of a self-governing people under a Constitution?

Or is it our people? Is it Americans who make us America?

Each is a part of the answer. President Ronald Reagan pulled these threads together and touched a chord with me and millions of others when he recast the words of Puritan John Winthrop into his sparkling phrase, "a shining city on a hill." For Americans like the Hassetts, with cherished ancestral memories of coming over from Ireland, President Reagan's striking image speaks directly to the hopes and dreams of forebears who made long journeys to American shores. People around the world look to this shining city on a hill and see a future they can hope for. That's why so many of us Americans count immigrants among our closest kin.

In his last speech as president, Ronald Reagan said, "A man wrote me and said: 'You can go to live in France, but you cannot become a Frenchman. You can go to live in Germany or Turkey or Japan, but you cannot become a German, a Turk, or a Japanese. But anyone, from any corner of the Earth, can come to live in America and become an American.'"[1]

In those few words, President Reagan made the point that to be an American is to subscribe to the American ideal, as well as to live in this physical place.

What President Reagan expressed in the 1980s, millions had responded to in the 1880s. There was nothing easy about it. The sheer difficulty of uprooting and immigrating to America with little wealth and no prospects was, in itself, a kind of a test. It was a test of imagination, hardiness, adventurousness, willingness to accept the hard work of starting over. It winnowed out people who didn't really want to be Americans. And for most of those who did, it was worth it. In the past, living in the shining city on a hill was something anyone in the world could aspire to if he wanted it badly enough.

Many saw Donald Trump's stance on immigration in comparison to Ronald Reagan's inspiring words and judged him to be coarse and callous, transactional, and lacking in idealism. But I came to see that Trump brought a perspective that complements Reagan's vision more than it contradicts it. Trump saw that immigration today is nothing like what it was in 1880 or 1950. Sixty-six percent of immigrants today come here because they are related to someone who has already migrated here. Another 22 percent get into the country because they were selected in a diversity lottery or for humanitarian reasons.[2] Many come here to get away from something, or to be a part of an expat community, not necessarily out of a burning desire to be an American.

And thus the image America presents to the world today is less that of a shining city on a hill and more like a big box store that opens its doors for a few minutes until the store is full. Then the doors are shut in people's faces until it is time for the next random influx of people. We've separated our ideas and ideals from our immigration policies. Our policies are heartless and stupid.

Donald Trump brought a much-needed frankness to the national dialogue about immigration policy. He reminded us that a country that doesn't control its borders is at risk of losing its identity and its existence as a nation. Laws that "wink" and encourage widespread non-enforcement, from Prohibition to our immigration laws, diminish respect for the rule of law. We have immigration policies that no other major country such as Canada, Mexico, France, or Australia would tolerate.

As I followed Donald Trump's candidacy, his criticisms, harsh and over the top as they sometimes were, forced me to sweep away the gauzy sentimentality that had built up in my mind and examine the effects of our current policies. As I engaged this issue, I wondered: Is there a way to reform the system so it can be idealistic and invitational, and yet maintain control over our borders and nationhood? Is it possible to have both the Reagan vision and the Trump practicality? While the question intrigued me, I never dreamed I would work on immigration. The hottest, most controversial issue throughout the Trump years was illegal immigration and "the Wall." I did my best to stay out of that conversation. The CEA was by statute non-partisan. As incredible as it may seem, Larry Summers and Paul Krugman, two giants of liberal economics, served in the CEA under President Reagan. More than once, my chief of staff would get a call from the White House press office "to make this tweet true." But if the president had tweeted out something incorrect, we were bound by law and professionalism not to try to spin facts to support it. I knew that the CEA chair's ability to move an agenda on issues like tax bills and deregulation depends on the agency's genuine commitment to independent analysis. It seemed it would be impossible to appear independent if I got caught up in the hyper-emotional immigration debates.

I even went so far as to kill a project that one of the CEA economists had dreamed up. If you build the Wall, he reasoned, then it would surely reduce drug trade. That would save American lives. If we apply a monetary value to those lives as the U.S. government does when it conducts cost-benefit analysis to decide, say, whether it makes sense to put up a guardrail, then the Wall would save thousands of lives and billions of dollars. In this sense, the Wall would pay for itself. It made empirical sense, but publishing that paper would have propelled us into a buzzsaw of emotional attacks and reduced or eliminated our chances to affect policy elsewhere. I felt a bit like the president must have felt when he ducked the Jones Act. I decided to stick with the better part of valor, discretion.

* * *

When I came to the White House, I was seen by my new peers as an establishment interloper on immigration. Steve Bannon and Peter Navarro had not missed that in my nomination hearings senators had tried to drive a wedge between me and the president on immigration. I confirmed that I tended more in the libertarian direction on immigration than the president's more restrictionist view. Frankly, a country has two choices. It can encourage immigration and have a relatively weak safety net for the poor, or it can have closed borders and a generous welfare state. The free-marketeer in me leans toward the former. President Trump leaned towards the latter. Democrats want to have it both ways and let the blurring outlines of America encourage the massive inflow of people dependent on the largesse of the state, a strategy that serves the Drift well.

This made me, in the eyes of some, a stripey-pants globalist establishment RINO. The lack of even the semblance of a policy process early on didn't help me find a constructive role for myself. In the first month, when Steve Bannon roamed around the Oval Office to tell the president not to follow my bad advice, it was far from clear whether our policy deliberations would even matter.

Early on the president advanced an immigration plan that was a non-starter in Congress. It was less about reforming and rethinking than simply reducing. Bannon had persuaded the president to cut legal immigration in half over a decade. As long as Democrats were relevant in Washington, D.C., that was never going to happen.

I found myself on a collision course with Stephen Miller, the speechwriter and policy advisor who somehow managed to become the éminence grise of the White House while still in his thirties. Stephen was especially suspicious of me. As he had so sharply reminded Gary Cohn and me in our meeting on steel, he was the keeper of the campaign promises.

Stephen was also a minister without portfolio—or rather, a minister with all domestic portfolios—popping in on meetings on trade, taxes, you name it. Stephen and Peter Navarro stood watch over the president's tariff policies. But immigration was Stephen's baby. He was determined to see the president's vision of closing off illegal immigration with the beloved Wall become reality. But he also helped mastermind more effective policies, such as keeping migrants in Mexico so they could not be caught by Customs and Border Patrol only to be released by the courts (never to appear again). Stephen expressed his passion for policy by using his gifts as a writer. Whenever you heard Donald Trump give a thoughtful policy speech read from a teleprompter, Stephen had written the speech—or at least massaged it. Work long enough in the White House, and you will realize that he who controls the pen defines the policy. Speechwriters literally get the last word.

As the economic and policy teams snapped into a cooperative pace on taxes and Bannon's White House tenure came to a close, the path was cleared for me to seek a better working relationship with Stephen on immigration. I set out to engage him on issues and to plumb his perspective. In one hallway conversation, Stephen and I discussed the prevailing view that America is suffering from a lack of STEM (Science, Technology, Engineering, and Mathematics) graduates, which leads naturally to the conclusion that the United States needs to recruit more STEM graduates from abroad.

Were high-skill immigrants, in fact, needed for these jobs?

When I mentioned the prevailing view that America did not have enough of such highly skilled people, Stephen gave me that flat, dead-eyed stare of his. He said, "Fake news, Kevin, not true." The smile that followed reflected Stephen's confidence that he was right, but also that he was warming to his new colleague.

I could have rejected what Stephen said. I am, after all, the economist. But instead, I told Stephen I'd look into it. Maybe he had a point.

I found that Americans who earn computer science degrees are almost all snapped up into a sector that is booming. But biologists? Physicists? Engineers? About 75 percent of STEM graduates were not getting final employment in their respective STEM field.[3] There are a lot of trade-offs and subtleties to be considered in this observation. But Stephen's assertion that many Americans were earning STEM degrees for which there were no jobs was basically true. (I suspect it is also true that many of these graduates also become disenchanted with decapitating rats and doing vector analysis of water flows.)

So I went back to Stephen and handed him CEA's analysis. I said, "You're right." He gave me a double take. Those are words you don't often hear in the staff quarters of the White House, but from that moment on a trust began to grow between us.

I made it a habit to drop by Stephen's office on the second floor of the West Wing. As we pulled together on trade and taxes, Stephen grew into his job and became more comfortable with the give-and-take of internal White House debates. With Steve Bannon no longer around to boycott meetings in which he couldn't win the argument, an orderly policy process began to take shape, and without Bannon's acting as an accelerant of suspicion, Stephen Miller quit picking fights and realized I was trying to help, not undermine him.

Stephen Miller has a reputation for being a tough guy with a steely gaze. But I came to see him as friendly and thoughtful. We were invited on one weekend retreat at Camp David in the Catoctin Mountains, a rare treat for senior staff. Imagine a luxurious but still rustic complex of log cabins with grey stone fireplaces and massive log beams, stuffed full of history. Camp David was the site of a Works Progress Administration camp, then called Shangri-la, that Winston Churchill visited as a guest of Franklin Delano Roosevelt. Dwight D. Eisenhower later renamed it for his grandson. It was where Jimmy Carter, Israeli Prime Minister Menachem Begin, and Egyptian President Anwar Sadat hammered out the Camp David Accords that brought a lasting peace between their nations. It was where Ronald Reagan planned Cold War strategy with Margaret Thatcher.

There is a Camp David cabin with the casual atmosphere of a mountain bar. There are plenty of beers on tap and a gift shop that sells cool Camp David memorabilia. Stephen and I had long conversations in that bar about taxes, trade, and immigration. We wound up drinking beer and playing shuffleboard and air hockey. I'm pretty good at games, but Stephen defeated me in air hockey every time. And he is a god of shuffleboard. I will say it outright: Stephen Miller is the Michael Jordan of shuffleboard.

In our conversations at Camp David and in Washington, Miller came to realize that I would be a player in immigration policy—no matter how much I initially shied away from touching the issue. It was my job to provide economic analysis on pieces of domestic policy. With this president constantly asking me to provide data on all sorts of issues, I soon knew that there was no way Donald Trump was going to leave me out of this centerpiece policy.

Donald Trump lit a constant fire underneath anyone who had a hand in the immigration portfolio. As long as progress was being made, the fire simmered. When he told a member of the Cabinet or sub-Cabinet to fix something and he or she failed to do so, the flame went on high. For example, after the president threatened to impose 25 percent tariffs on Mexico, there was a lag before Mexico began to slow the caravans and contain them. In this early phase, Kirstjen Nielsen, then secretary of Homeland Security, did not have a crisp answer when the president asked her in a Cabinet meeting about news reports that we were about to lose control of the border.

"It's your job to secure the border!" the president shouted at her. "What the hell are you doing over there!" He tore into her in front of the Cabinet in a way that made everyone look down at their writing pads. None of us wanted to get that treatment.

When Donald Trump was passionate about something, he would first calmly tell a Cabinet secretary or staff to fix it. If it wasn't fixed the next time he saw that secretary, all his earlier patience went out the window. This was a strength and a weakness. Intense pressure can produce results from secretaries trying to corral torpid and resistant bureaucracies. But all presidents must face chronic, long-term problems that take time to maneuver. Steven Mnuchin and Wilbur Ross knew how to manage the president and to anticipate his demands. For those who didn't, Donald Trump's frustration would boil over into rage. This was one reason why Cabinet secretaries came and went like temps.

For the Camp David retreat, I suggested to Ivanka that the president must really love the wilderness retreat. "My dad is not a hiker," she said, "in fact there is zero chance he would ever do anything outdoorsy." But he came up to spend an afternoon with us, casually talking with us in the main dining building, and then holding an impromptu senior staff meeting in the giant conference room next to the dining room. True to form, one of the first things he did was announce to us all that he was really fed up with a certain Cabinet secretary and asked each of us to vote on whether that person should be fired.

★ ★ ★

In 2019, as he was facing re-election, the president's frustration with the lack of progress on immigration was palpable. To develop a detailed and realistic immigration reform plan would require coordinating the various tribes of Republicans on Capitol Hill—restrictionists and immigration enthusiasts—as well as the business lobby clamoring for more labor, the Trump base clamoring to shut it off, and Republican Hispanic and Asian leaders wanting both reform and respect.

Such a job would require finesse. So, as he did time and again, Trump tasked Jared Kushner with pulling these threads together into a coherent plan, strategically developed with appeals to varied constituencies. Stephen Miller was not happy about relinquishing the reins to Jared, but he recognized the wisdom of using Jared's organizational talents.

"Let's put a fresh set of eyes to immigration and see what we can do to solve this problem," the president told Jared. So the president's son-in-law asked Stephen and me to come up with a plan to dramatically recast American immigration policy. Our focus extended far beyond border security to envision a whole reboot of the system.

Jared, like his father-in-law, has a businessman's ability to see fundamental issues in a way that causes him to reject tinkering in favor of wholesale rethinking. He enlisted us in a top to bottom reimagining of how immigration should work.

How could we get beyond the impersonal and irrational admittance policy to something that made sense both for would-be immigrants and for the United States? How could we restore the vision of an America that immigrants would strive to move to? How could we once again see ourselves as the shining city on a hill?

Imagine you're a young person living in Ghana and you dream of moving to the United States. Unless you have relatives living here, it is virtually impossible. But what if we had a merit-based system in which a young person, anywhere in the world, could aspire to become an American if they followed the rules and applied themselves? What if we had a system in which one didn't luck out by family circumstances or a lottery, but had to qualify to become an American?

Our idea was for that young person to go to a website or a consulate, type in the basics of his or her life experience, education, work history, and goals. This process would be interactive. If you are earning a bachelor's degree in Accra, Ghana, you might be encouraged to finish your degree and apply again. If you live in Phnom Penh, Cambodia, know English, but are not quite proficient, you might be asked to improve. And you would be tested on your knowledge of America *before* being accepted. Why is it that we give immigrants a citizenship test after they've arrived? Why not task would-be immigrants with learning about the Revolution, the Constitution, the Fourteenth Amendment, and World War II while they're still abroad? Why not have them write an essay on why they want to come to America?

The United States should attract people with drive, who are highly skilled and who contribute to our country and economy. A merit system does exactly this. We surveyed the world's immigration policies and found that Canada and Australia have merit systems for immigrants that have worked well for the citizens of those countries. Such a system would also be fair instead of random. It would not be the door of a big box store swinging open for a few minutes. It would spell out what you need to do to get here.

Consider: The United States admits 12 percent of our immigrants on the basis of employment and skills, while 63 percent of people admitted by Canada and 68 percent of people admitted by Australia are admitted for skills they contribute to these countries.[4] It is a truism of economics that immigrants add to a country's wealth and job growth. But educated, skilled, and motivated immigrants would be Miracle-Gro for the U.S. economy.

We presented our plan to the president, one that—after border security and the inspection of all people and scanning of 100 percent of goods at points of entry—included a new and better system for immigrants. Asylum seekers would face a quicker and more rational process, which closed loopholes and eliminated fraudulent abuses of the system while providing due process. Border crossers would face quicker and more certain removal.

The part I had worked on would place America in the global race for talent, to enhance our competitiveness and grow our economy and jobs. We proposed a new "Build America VISA," a point-based application system for applicants in high-skill categories who would take front-end civics tests. This front-end civics test would gauge an applicant's ability to engage the ideas of American history and their appreciation of the American ideal. The test would also consider age, health, English proficiency, educational and vocational certificates, possible criminal backgrounds, and other qualities in an applicant. Only 42 percent of immigrants in our current system have a bachelor's or advanced degree. Our proposal would up that percentage to 71 percent. Under our proposed system, the annual wages of new immigrants would double from $43,000 to $96,000. These new Americans would add $600 billion to our economy in ten years and increase tax revenues by $500 billion over a decade.[5]

"We can attract the best and brightest, those who could flourish socially and economically in our country," I told the president. "Our plan will ensure that everybody who comes to America actually wants to be an American."

Among those in this briefing with me were Jared and Stephen Miller. I was glad for the company, because I went into the Oval Office with no small trepidation. Would the president judge me to be a globalist wimp? As I spoke, I could see that Donald Trump understood what we were saying. By the time I finished, I was beaming. We were getting to a place where the president who was so tough on the Wall and the caravans could also see how we could once again be the shining city on a hill.

"You know, this is fantastic," he said to us. "This is the best immigration reform I've ever seen. I can even see that if we did it right, we could even raise the number of immigrants we let in if we wanted to. So let's do it."

He turned somber.

"We can't get it passed with Nancy Pelosi trying to impeach me. But it's not too early to start to build a drumbeat of support for it after the next election. It will be the first thing I do when we win."

Jared and I took our PowerPoint presentation to the *Washington Post* editorial board. Stephen was skeptical about going to a newspaper that was so relentlessly critical of the president, but he signed off on the idea. The *Post*'s editors were friendly, skeptical as you would expect, but ready to listen. A few days later, they issued their verdict.

> President Trump's proposal to overhaul the legal immigration system by favoring educated, skilled English speakers with strong earnings prospects over relatives of current residents represents an improvement over the administration's previous bar-the-door approach. . . . The blueprint attempts to forge a consensus in the Republican Party to continue the flow of legal immigrants at current levels. That would be welcome, because immigrants are wellsprings of energy, ambition and pluck who have enriched this country and will remain essential to its prosperity.[6]

The plan, of course, became inoperable once Donald Trump lost his bid for re-election. But it remains in place and deserves to be a centerpiece discussion in the 2024 Republican presidential debates. And President Biden, should he want to make progress on this tricky issue, could start with a bill that President Trump loved and add his own touches.

When the time comes to push the bill, proponents need to be fully aware of the crucial place that immigration holds in the process that is the Drift towards socialism. Immigration fights are so nasty because immigration is so crucial to the Drift. If we allow more and more hard-working entrepreneurs into the country, people educated abroad, at universities not run by Marxists, then the set of people with strong faith in the traditional American economic system will expand and those smart immigrants will drive up the productivity and wages of low-skilled Americans, making them less open to the idea of socialism. But if immigration allows in a massive wave of low-skilled wards of the state, then the set of people willing to view the state as a beneficent nanny will increase. To the extent that the low-skilled immigrants work, this will drive down the wages of low-skilled American citizens as well, creating an even bigger customer base for socialism.

The irony of Stephen and my working together on immigration was not lost on Washington. As Jared Kushner told *The Hill*, "If I can get Kevin Hassett and Stephen Miller to agree on an immigration plan, Middle East peace will be easy by comparison."[7]

As it turned out, a Middle East peace deal, at least the long-sought Arab–Israeli peace agreement, was in fact more achievable than a new immigration plan for the United States. And in short order, it happened.

## CHAPTER NINE

# The Fruits of Leverage Diplomacy

If immigration is America's most intractable issue, the hostility between the Arab states and Israel over the status of the Palestinian people has long been seen as the most intractable quarrel in the world. From the end of the British Mandate through the Six-Day and Yom Kippur Wars, to the intifada, it has been a given that Arabs and Jews will forever be at each other's throats. President Jimmy Carter's Camp David Accords did bring about peace between Israel and Egypt, but the truculent peace based on common interests was not the real peace of two neighbors helping each other thrive.

Successive administrations sought a lasting solution for the Palestinians, and therefore an end to Arab and Israeli hostility, through interminable discussions in Oslo, Madrid, and other venues. Amid the pomp, toasts, and hors d'oeuvres, there was always an air of morbid fatalism to these talks. Only once did it seem a breakthrough would occur. This happened under the auspices of President Bill Clinton when Israeli Prime Minister Ehud Barak held direct talks with Palestinian leader Yasser Arafat at Camp David. The prime minister practically chased Arafat around the table, offering him one concession after another. Barak later said Bill Clinton told him, "The true story of Camp David was that for the first time in the history of the conflict the American president put on the table a proposal, based on UN Security Council resolutions 242 and 338, very close to the Palestinian demands, and Arafat refused even to accept it as a basis for negotiations, walked out of the room, and deliberately turned to terrorism."[1]

In the memorable and commonly cited paraphrase of the great Israeli statesman Abba Eban, the Palestinians "never miss an opportunity to miss an opportunity."[2]

The world looked on and despaired. Donald Trump surveyed this scene and saw enormous potential. He dispatched Jared Kushner and confirmed that several tectonic shifts had taken place, little appreciated by American and European diplomats as they clinked their glasses and dined off fine china.

The first shift was that the leaders of the emirates and kingdoms of the Arab states had developed an ambition to invest their trillions of petrodollars to fund a transition in the Arab world toward education, science, and manufacturing. They admired the Jewish state and saw in it an opportunity for a fruitful collaboration between their talent and capital and those of their neighbor.

The second shift was that the Arab leaders had become disgusted by the incompetence, corruption, and intractability of Fatah in the West Bank and Hamas in Gaza.

Third, the Sunni Arab states had come to see Shia Iran and its nuclear ambitions as a mortal threat. No sleep was lost in the Arab capitals over Israel's sizable nuclear arsenal; considerable sleep has been lost over the continuing efforts of the radical mullahs in Tehran to develop an arsenal that would make Iran a regional superpower.

Iran had long had a proxy in the radical Shia Hezbollah militia to bedevil Israel from the north, just as Iranian-backed militias frequently fire missiles into Israel from Gaza in the south. It did not go unnoticed in the Arab capitals that Iran had become the principal backer and puppeteer of Hamas in Gaza, providing stipends and weaponry. Meanwhile,

Iran funds Yemen's Houthi rebels, alarming the Saudis to their immediate north.

Like Richard Nixon, the first president to exploit the deep divisions between the Soviet Union and the People's Republic of China, Donald Trump was the first to see that the Iranian threat provided a wedge for diplomacy. He appreciated, from personal diplomacy, that a nuclear-armed Iran is the nightmare that keeps leaders awake at night in Cairo, Riyadh, and Abu Dhabi. For an Arab leader, a powerful, nuclear-armed Israeli state was beginning to look like a stabilizing factor. Or, as an ancient Muslim proverb goes: your friends are three—your friend, your friend's friend, and the enemy of your enemy.

A fourth shift was the growing appreciation for the Palestinian people—long treated as pawns by world leaders, including their own—as a resilient, increasingly educated people, desirous not just of a state of their own, but for a way to employ their talents to build a better future.

Trump saw all this and to his credit began to reap the benefits of the tectonic shifts that had occurred in the Middle East.

Most presidents would prepare for peacemaking by offering sweeteners and concessions. President Trump's blunt and domineering approach proved better suited to the mindset of the Middle East. He first demonstrated the depth of America's relationship with Israel. He did what past presidents had promised but never done, approving the move of the U.S. embassy from Tel Aviv to Jerusalem.

The conventional wisdom held that such a move would inflame the proverbial "Arab street." It did not. Donald Trump sent Palestinian diplomats in Washington packing and cut their aid. The Arab street yawned. The sense of solidarity the Arab nations had with the Palestinians had been eroded by their refusal to deal as honest brokers, their corruption, and their willingness to serve as agents of Iranian influence. Trump exposed this rift.

Meanwhile, Trump had replaced the ineffectual Rex Tillerson at the State Department with the more focused Mike Pompeo. Contemptuous of Obama's nuclear weapons deal with Tehran, Trump ignored the entreaties of European allies and instructed Pompeo and Mnuchin to double down on sanctions on Iran. In early 2020, he ordered a drone strike to kill Iranian general and national hero Qasem Soleimani as he left the Baghdad airport. This was an astonishingly brazen exercise of American power. It was also justified. Soleimani had masterminded the killing of hundreds of American soldiers through proxies in Iraq, as well as fomented unrest and armed conflict throughout the region.

The assassination of Soleimani was a bold stroke that shocked the Iranians to the core. It convinced Saudi Arabia and the emirates that Trump was a dependable ally. Trump instinctively understood that the Middle East respects strength, not insipid goodwill. And while Washington reviled and ridiculed him, Trump had established credibility in the Middle East while exposing the fault lines and opportunities in the region.

★ ★ ★

One morning, Jared Kushner dropped by my office. Jared is such a gentle-spirited and unassuming guy that he had no problem walking over to the CEA even though his office, right next to the Oval Office, was the most prime real estate in the White House. Jared told me that with the bold moves Trump had made in favor of Israel, the president had unprecedented political capital to spend with the Israelis. By taking equally bold actions against Iran, the president also had unprecedented leverage with leading Arab states. He calmly explained the situation, outlining the fundamental realities in a logical way. This was classic Jared, someone who sees the underlying currents and describes them in a direct, toned-down way that instills confidence. Donald Trump always turned the knob to eleven, which sometimes inspired you to act with urgency but also made you want to tune him out. Kushner's soft-spoken confidences made you want to lean in and absorb every word he was saying. He was a useful and welcome complement to the president's high-strung energy.

As I talked with Jared, the president, Steven Mnuchin, and others, we saw that any Middle East peace deal would need to address the untapped potential—ignored by the world and the Palestinian leadership alike—of the 4.5 million Palestinian people. The per capita wealth of the Palestinian people is less than half that of the other people of the Middle East and North Africa. The West Bank, notably poor compared to other Arab societies, is a bright spot compared to the abysmal poverty of Gaza. The per capita income of Palestinians in the West Bank and Gaza together was well below that of Sri Lanka, Tuvalu, and the Republic of the Congo. Capital is scarce, and industrial output is low in the Palestinian areas. Only 25 percent of Gaza's whole population is employed, compared to 34 percent in war-torn Yemen and 50 percent in the rest of the Arab League.[3]

So we approached the problem of Palestinian poverty, and the terrorism it generates and the terrorists it cultivates, in the same way we approached enterprise zones and immigration: by appreciating the potential of disadvantaged people. After these discussions, I placed a call to Peru. I invited a colleague and friend, a Peruvian economist with the name of a conquistador, Hernando de Soto, to lunch at the White House to speak with our economics and Middle East team.

Hernando is a large man with a kind face and a deliberate, winning manner. He addressed the team in Jared's office by telling us how to utterly upend the dynamic of terror and strife in the Middle East by unlocking the talents of the Palestinian people. He began to tell a story, familiar to me, that left the team, especially Jared, entranced.

In the late 1980s, Hernando said, he had advanced what was then a novel theory, one immediately recognized as a brilliant summation of a truth that had gone largely unrecognized. He asserted that there are *trillions* of dollars' worth of capital locked up in businesses owned by small entrepreneurs in poor countries. In Peru, for example, small entrepreneurs account for 62 percent of that country's population, generate almost a third of the country's wealth, and hold $70 billion in that country's real-estate assets.[4]

But there was a problem that Hernando and his graduate students demonstrated in an ingenious experiment. He set up a small garment business with sewing machines in a Lima slum. Then he dispatched his graduate students to government offices to fill out every form needed to obtain every license required to legally operate that business, without paying a céntimo in bribes. As it turned out, it could be done. A legal business could be opened in Peru with all the forms completed and stamped without bribes. It only took 289 days to do it.

Only an economist with an academic grant, of course, could afford to do that. When small business owners cannot obtain a legal title to their business, it means that they must operate in a legal gray zone. No bank will give them a loan to expand their business or buy new equipment because no land or building or equipment they "own" can be considered collateral, and they have to pay bribes to any policeman or inspector who comes calling threatening to shut down their "illegal" business.

This, Hernando pointed out, is exactly what happened to Mohamed Bouazizi, a twenty-six-year-old Tunisian man who had built up a business of fruit and vegetable stands. In 2010, inspectors looking for payoffs had confiscated Bouazizi's merchandise and scale. The last straw for Bouazizi came when a municipal inspector slapped him across the face.[5] The young man responded to his despair and humiliation by going on social media, setting himself on fire, and burning himself to death.

In the wake of his death, dozens of men and women in Algeria, Morocco, Saudi Arabia, Tunisia, and Yemen also set fire to themselves. The social-media reaction, known today as the Arab Spring, was an earthquake that shook every Arab government to its foundations. Four regimes were toppled. Hernando spoke movingly of the many individual tragedies contained in the great currents of history. He left the White House Middle East team in tears all around, but more importantly with a grim determination to help make life better for the Bouazizis of the world.

Bouazizi was the kind of person every society should value. He had started his business at age twelve and built it up into something to be proud of. But his enterprise always operated on the edge of confiscation from bribe-seekers and their harassment. He could not even sell off his business because he did not really own it.

Bouazizi had what Hernando calls "dead" capital, wealth that cannot be accessed, used as collateral, or transferred because it does not exist legally. Hernando estimates that in Egypt alone, small business owners hold $360 billion of dead capital lacking legal recognition. "That amounts," Hernando wrote in the *Wall Street Journal*, "to roughly a hundred times more than what the West is going to give to Egypt this year in financial, military and development assistance—and eight times more than the value of all foreign direct investment in Egypt since Napoleon invaded more than 200 years ago."[6]

So forget oil. The oceans of underground wealth in the Middle East are to be found in souks and shopping malls. Could this wealth be legalized? What would the economic and political results of doing that be? Since Aristotle, thinkers have realized that the development of a strong middle class is essential to a functioning democracy. If this dead capital could become viable, would that stabilize this notoriously unstable region?

Hernando told us it could because he had already done it in Peru.

In the 1990s, Peru's government was fighting for its life against a Marxist terrorist militia called the Shining Path, which had effective control over most of the country. Hernando became a principal advisor to the Peruvian president and persuaded the government to reduce red tape by 75 percent and encouraged legislation that gave official recognition to informal businesses by the hundreds of thousands. Legal reform allowed Peru to grow its gross national product per capita twice as fast as the rest of the Latin American average. The Peruvian middle class burgeoned.[7] The success of these policies isolated the Shining Path, which set the stage for a U.S.-backed effort largely to defeat Shining Path with more economic reform and a military campaign enthusiastically backed by the people.

It wasn't easy. Municipal and local officials did not like the fact that de Soto and his followers in government wanted to curtail their pipeline of bribes. The Shining Path tried to kill Hernando with a bomb that, he said, caused the floor of a government ministry to rise five inches. But in the end they lost, and Peru's new middle class won.

I could see Jared and the others grow fidgety as Hernando spoke, not because he bored them, but because he fired them up. It was clear that the path to a permanent and fruitful peace in the Middle East would include the liberation of human ambition in Palestine. We were going to do for the Palestinian people what Hernando did for Peru. We were going to rescue them from the Drift.

\* \* \*

"I'm nervous and hopeful at the same time," I said. It was a few months after our meeting with Hernando.

Steven Mnuchin and Jared nodded. We were nursing beers in a pub at the Shannon Airport. For some reason, I ended up paying for the beers even though I was the poorest guy in the room. Outside, our military jet was being refueled in the rain for the next leg of our trip to Bahrain. We had spent almost all of our time since Hernando's meeting devising a detailed White House plan to deliver prosperity to the Palestinian people. There were two seats that folded down into beds in the middle of the jet. These were reserved by protocol for Steven and Jared. The rest of us were in very comfortable seats that recline about halfway.

We had all poured our faith and hard work into backing economic and humanitarian deals between the Arab states and Israel. Economic considerations are often ancillary side deals to peace agreements. We thought of the economics side as the centerpiece. And we put our money, so to speak, where our mouths were. We had a plan that was detailed down to hundreds of specific projects that would lift Palestinians out of poverty. And we had people in the room, leaders of the Arab nations, who were willing to finance our plan. Were we being dangerously naïve? We had not consulted the Palestinian authorities, at least not in any substantive way, in designing our plan for their people. But I insisted to the team that this was an acceptable approach. Good ideas and solid analysis eventually win hearts and minds. If the Palestinians took our report and enacted it themselves, we would all be happy for their people, even if they never gave us any credit for designing the projects.

The Palestinian Authority was boycotting the "Peace to Prosperity: A Vision to Improve the Lives of the Palestinian and Israeli People" conference at which we would unveil our proposal sponsored by the crown prince of Bahrain. The Israeli government was also not attending. There was a rumor that the Palestinian Authority would send a representative, but they did not, a classic Palestinian Authority blunder. They truly do never miss a chance to miss a chance!

Egypt and Morocco, though participating, sent mid-level representatives. We were setting out a plan for two nations whose governments were not official participants. How would that be received?

Manama is an island kingdom in the Persian Gulf separated from Saudi Arabia by a causeway. On the drive in, I saw that Manama lives up to its reputation as a gorgeous city of high rises, date palms, and white-sand beaches stretching along turquoise waters. All participants were guests of the kingdom's crown prince. Delegates from Dubai, Saudi Arabia, and the Gulf emirates were in attendance, with others from Australia, Nigeria, and Norway—some 300 in all.[8]

Our hotel, the Four Seasons, is a high-tech, high-rise modernist work of art. Our sessions in the Four Seasons's banquet hall were well produced extravaganzas worthy of Hollywood or a TED Talk. But if you stepped outside, it was as hot as a human can possibly handle. Our rooms were as nice as any I have ever seen, and the hosts had arranged for generous gift baskets for all of us with fancy candies and bottles of perfume. Figuring some ethics officer somewhere would send me to prison, I left the basket there, but I confess that I did eat some of the chocolates.

Jared Kushner spoke early, establishing himself as the quarterback of the event. "To be clear," he said, addressing the absent Palestinians, "economic growth and prosperity for the Palestinian people are not possible without an enduring and fair political solution to the conflict—one that guarantees Israel's security and respects the dignity of the Palestinian people." He made the point that an "economic pathway" is necessary to establishing the preconditions for peace.[9]

Then Jared took aim at the Palestinian Authority: "My direct message to the Palestinian people is that despite what those who have let you down in the past say, President Trump and America have not given up on you." He set out a compelling vision of "a bustling commercial and tourist center in Gaza and the West Bank, where international businesses come together and thrive."[10]

The annual budget of the Palestinian Authority is about $2 billion.[11] Steven Mnuchin and Jared Kushner touted $50 billion in grant money, low-interest loans, and private capital as part of its investment strategy for the West Bank, Gaza, and neighboring Arab nations.[12] Stephen Schwartzman, CEO of the Blackstone Group, stressed how doable it was to raise that amount of money from Western and Arab sources "for remaking a region."[13] AT&T CEO Randall Stephenson spoke about how just one sector of the economy, telecommunications, could easily be transformed in a way that would positively affect all Palestinians. He noted that Palestinians, lacking their own cell network, have to rely on service from Israel. Stephenson spoke of industry's capacity to get twenty-first-century telecom infrastructure up and running quickly for Palestinians. Palestinian businessman Ashraf Jabari, who works hand-in-glove with Jewish settlers, spoke of the potential for Israelis and Palestinians to thrive together.

If realized, the plan would implement 190 projects to clear the bottleneck that holds the Palestinians back. The plan would make electricity reliable, double the supply of drinkable water, connect more Palestinian schools to high-speed data services, encourage the participation of more women in the work force, and connect the West Bank and Gaza with a high-speed rail corridor.

To fully realize the economic plan, Jared acknowledged that political deals would be needed. But it was time to move on from the failed diplomatic policies of the past. "Enough of the old broken record," he said.[14]

When I spoke, I held up the 180-page White House plan and its careful, detailed suggestions that so many others had spoken from. My strongest point came from data points that should outrage anyone—the shocking condition of the underperforming economy of Palestine and poverty of the people compared to the entrepreneurial drive and talent the people possess. The CEA staff made a chart that showed per capita national income for countries around the world and related it to the literacy rate of the country. The relationship was strong and convincing. Countries that are literate have much higher incomes. But in the chart, there was one striking outlier: Palestine. It is one of the most literate and well-educated countries on earth but has one of the lowest average incomes. There was so much tragedy and so much promise, and our enthusiasm about that promise spread throughout the conference.

At a lunch with crown princes and the like, Jared sat me at the middle of the table, and we handed around economic slides to convince everyone that we had a plan that would work. I will always believe that that lunch is where the peace deal happened. We genuinely worked to produce a plan that would unquestionably help the Palestinian people, and their leaders failed to show. The Arab leaders understood that their love and support of the Palestinian people required them morally to divorce from a leadership that was as resistant to positive change as the Shining Path terrorists that Hernando De Soto had defeated. Really, it was another appearance of the Drift. The Marxists of the Shining Path were defeated by capitalism. The socialists running Palestine into the ground had created an enormous capitalist opportunity if only the Palestinians would take it.

The event ended with a breakthrough. The closing panel, led by Steven Mnuchin, culminated in the finance ministers from the Gulf countries and the Bahrain foreign minister's proclaiming: "Israel is a country in the region, and it is there to stay, of course. As much as Camp David was a major game-changer. . . . If this succeeds, and we build on it, and it attracts attention and momentum, this would be the second game-changer."[15]

As they spoke, I noticed Crown Prince Salman bin Hamad Ahmed Al Khalifa of Bahrain smiling and nodding in agreement.

It was the high point in my career at the White House and one of the most inspiring moments of my life. It set the basis for the signing of the Abraham Accords in August by the United Arab Emirates, and Israel in September. Sudan followed with a normalization agreement, as did Morocco (after President Trump made the controversial decision to recognize Morocco's claims in the Western Sahara).

In September, Jared Kushner called to invite me as a VIP guest to the signing ceremony of the Abraham Accords. I stood watching President Trump and Israeli Prime Minister Benjamin Netanyahu join the UAE foreign minister and Bahraini foreign minister to give remarks from the South Portico of the White House.

When Netanyahu spoke, he referred to the accords as a "pivot of history." But he also dwelled at length on the loss of his brother, Yonatan, and other Israeli "victims of terror" in fighting terrorists. Beyond a few bromides, the prime minister's remarks lacked the celebratory graciousness and magnanimity such a moment required. He gave a speech that seemed packaged for a domestic audience that tracked how hard it was to make a deal with countries with which Israel had long enmity without acknowledging the difficulty and risks taken by the other side.

I could sense that he made many in the audience uncomfortable. I was appalled.

But then the president stepped up to the historic moment.

"This could lead to peace, real peace in the Middle East for the first time," Trump said of the accords, shortly before losing his second bid for office. "We've taken a very different path. You could say it's a backdoor, but I call it a smart door."[16]

The early signs from the Biden administration are that it is back to the future in the Middle East. The administration shows every sign of reviving Barack Obama's failed policy of appeasing Iran while treating the historic breakthrough of the Abraham Accords as something unfortunate left on a prize rug by the family pet. Their vision of a socialist

America would be harder to achieve if capitalism saved Palestine as it did Peru, so I feel certain the Abraham Accords will bear a target until Biden and his team are gone.

The Biden administration has also put under review the Trump plan to sell fifty F-35 jet fighters to the UAE. For the larger Abraham Accords, however, it may be that the United States has started a process in which we are no longer needed. The Emirates are eagerly expanding the economic dimensions of their deal with Israel. They are not going to stop because President Joe Biden and Secretary of State Antony Blinken are unenthusiastic. This deal has a dynamic of its own.

★ ★ ★

If there is one common theme running throughout my work in the White House—from tax cuts to enterprise zones, from a skills- and education-based focus on immigration to a plan for the Palestinian people—the centerpiece concern has always been the liberation of human talent, ingenuity, and imagination. Such an optimistic belief in the potential of the individual is anathema and antidote to the Drift of socialism. The owner of a small shop, nail salon, printing store, or internet café has the entrepreneurial guile and mettle that we as a nation should cultivate and encourage. The poor town I grew up in showed me how undeserving the people around me were of the suffering they endured. Economics is a powerful tool, and I felt called to use it to try to make the world a better place.

While the immigration plan and the Palestinian peace plan are sidelined, they are not dead. They can't die because they are based on timeless ideas. These deals targeted the hardworking people around the world who are the heart and soul of the global economy. When government no longer leads, when it becomes an obstacle, it must get out of their way. These plans are waiting for the next disruptor to dust them off and put them into action.

* * *

In my last months at CEA, Mick Mulvaney became the acting chief of staff. He had been offered his dream job, the presidency of the University of South Carolina. When he told President Trump he intended to leave, Donald Trump looked up at him and said, "Why don't you become my chief of staff, instead?"

The elevation of Mulvaney to replace General Kelly was a needed change, just as Kelly's selection had been an improvement over Priebus. Each man brought unique skills. Each struggled in his own way to fill the president's shifting needs. Kelly's mode of operation was to keep President Trump from doing something reckless. Mick brought a more positive spin to the task—to help the president achieve items on his agenda in a smart way. He also brought a needed sense of play.

Mick and I shared an Irish sense of the absurd, alleviated by a slight tipple now and then. As director of the Office for Management and Budget (OMB), Mick held a Friday night keg party where interns and senior staffers mingled in the interior patio of the Old Executive Office building. To remind himself of his native South Carolina, Mick imported a huge Palmetto tree. (It was too big to be brought up the stairs, and it died.) He kept a huge popcorn machine in OMB and invited anyone in the administration to come by and scoop their own. When he took over the chief of staff's office next to the Oval Office, Mick brought the machine and the scent of fresh popcorn into the West Wing.

It made sense. After all, if the Trump White House was going to be such a theatrical spectacle, why not have popcorn?

A little levity helps, especially in the fevered White House atmosphere where everything is always considered a crisis. When we first put out our Economic Report of the President, among the many interns we thanked at the end in small type were "J. T. Kirk" and "J. L. Picard." In a latter edition, we added, "Bruce Wayne, Aunt May, and Peter Parker." Part of our point was to run an experiment. If we added heroes from *Star Trek* and D.C. and Marvel comics, would anybody notice? Jim Tankersley of the *New York Times* finally did and wrote a bemused piece about our "Comic-Con Easter Egg." We tweeted out: "Thank you for noticing, our interns are indeed superheroes!"

In the ensuing tweetstorm, however, tweeters started assuming that names of actual interns we thanked, people with good old Anglo-Saxon cognates in them that sounded like common words for body parts, or were evocative of certain sex acts, were our dirty double-entendres . . . well we then realized we had had enough fun with that. Time to stop.

"Have a sense of humor," our spokeswoman said to Tankersley.

"Funny," he wrote in his piece, "that's what people usually say to economists."[17]

I had had a lot of fun. But I had had enough. I was, from the start, in a weird position. I was always supposed to be the adult in the room, but I found my established opinions challenged and even changed by Donald Trump's fresh take on everything. I was trusted by the president but constantly parrying attacks from colleagues and the media. It was exhausting.

Most CEA chairmen serve for about two years. As the head of an agency, the CEA chair is tasked with being a neutral presenter of objective economic facts. My role was to help the administration make plans, from tariffs to tax cuts, by projecting likely outcomes of given policies. While I was a key part of the economic team, my post did not permit me to be a policy "player" in the sense that Steven Mnuchin, Gary Cohn, and Larry Kudlow could be. This was a role I was comfortable playing, but it was not a role that others could not do. I was happy to serve until the summer of 2019, succeeded by two strong deputies, Tomas Philipson and, when Tomas returned to his post at the University of Chicago, by Tyler Goodspeed.

I joined my CEA predecessor and friend Larry Lindsey in a private business. But, to quote Al Pacino as Michael Corleone, "Just when I think I'm out, they pull me back in." With the emergence of the coronavirus in early 2020, the president wanted me back by his side. I took a ninety-day appointment that would allow me to work in the West Wing, suspending outside business, but without having to permanently resign from those business and board positions I had accepted after leaving the White House.

The fact that I was called back to have an office in the West Wing and be at the center of the White House response to the COVID crisis is perhaps the best metric of the journey I took in the White House. When he was elected, President Trump said he didn't like economists, and the CEA was kicked out of the Cabinet. When I arrived, I was the globalist asshole who was so controversial that the president had to call me to his office and tell me he had my back. And by the end, the fact-driven data analysis our staff delivered day-in and day-out had won so many converts that the president called me back to advise him on managing the economic impact of the COVID crisis.

And behind all that is the gradual realization that we were all fighting against a force bigger than ourselves, fighting against the Drift.

## CHAPTER TEN

# Socialism and Trump's Place in History

Millions worry about America's Drift toward "socialism," but what is it exactly? What does this word mean to the millennials who would welcome it? What would it actually be if enacted? And would that really be so bad?

Gallup reports that the largest response from Americans polled in 1949, when asked about their understanding of socialism, defined it as government ownership or control of business. Most Americans today respond that socialism means greater economic equality, or the provision of free benefits like health care. For some, it is just a synonym for "liberalism."[1]

When I served as chair of President Trump's CEA in October 2018, we grappled with the question of defining socialism. We did so because of the radical influences growing within the Democratic party. The nature of socialism was no longer an academic question. With progressives taking over one of the nation's two parties, socialism could actually happen in America. So the CEA produced a report about socialism and its social costs. In the first half of this chapter, I will review many of the main points raised in our report.

Our report concluded that socialism had two defining characteristics:

> Whether a country or industry is socialist is a question of the
> degree to which (a) the means of production, distribution, and
> exchange are owned or regulated by the state; and (b) the state
> uses its control to distribute the economic output without
> regard for final consumers' willingness to pay or exchange
> (i.e., giving resources away "for free").[2]

To put it in non-wonky terms, socialism is an economic system in which the government controls how stuff gets made. There are two categories of stuff that make stuff. Marxists call one category "the means of production." We call it "capital"—the money and equipment required to realize a business vision. The second category is labor, the humans in the chain of production. You need both the living humans, labor, and inanimate objects and financing, capital, to make the stuff that people want and need.

In a socialist system, the government can control the means of production in two ways. One is by controlling the supply of goods by controlling the major decisions of businesses and capital. Some governments, like the People's Republic of China, take this approach. China's willingness to intervene on the supply side can be seen in the government's decision to take over a big portion of the financial services giant Ant on the eve of its IPO after its founder, Jack Ma, made a speech mildly critical of the government. This should not be a surprise to anyone, yet somehow it continues to surprise China-friendly, Davos-centered Western elites. Xi Jinping continues to extol the virtues of socialism in a body of writings—with a hat tip to Chairman Mao—called "Xi Jinping Thought on Socialism with Chinese Characteristics for a New Era."[3] "When somebody shows you who they are," wrote Maya Angelou, "believe them the first time."[4] Ever since the Tiananmen Square massacre, the Chinese Communist Party has not only been showing us, but actively trying to tell us what socialism with Chinese characteristics is.

The second way to have socialism is to let the supply side govern itself while intervening extensively on the demand side of the economy. This is done by providing necessities like health care, childcare, housing, and food free of charge. This is the path the Nordic countries took in the 1970s.

Then there are communist countries that do both. They practice socialism from top to bottom. In Cuba and Venezuela today, the government controls all capital, all labor, all supply, and all demand. These countries, like the old Soviet Union and China under Chairman Mao, are, not surprisingly, the most oppressive.

Where does the United States fit on this spectrum? We have extensive regulations on capital, finance, and labor, with a tax code that further regulates and distorts the market. There is considerable provision of government health care, childcare, housing, and food to the poor. Overall, however, we still have a robust capitalist system. The Fraser Institute, a free market think tank in Canada, compiles an economic freedom index of the world's nations, ranking states from first (Hong Kong) to last (Venezuela) in terms of the freedom to enter and compete in those markets, as well as the legal protection of people and property and other factors. One can presume that Hong Kong's ranking will tank given China's "Anschluss."

In 2014, under the Obama administration, the United States ranked sixteenth, behind Mauritius and the United Arab Emirates on the Economic Freedom Index.[5] This was a significant downgrade from sixth place when George W. Bush left office in 2008. Just two years into the Trump administration, the administration's policies had the United States back to sixth place again.[6] Expect the economic freedom ranking of the United States to drop as the Biden administration reinstates regulations lifted during the last four years. As we march down the rankings, we head toward a world where government control reaches into every corner of our lives. History shows that socialism always degrades a country, making its people poorer and sapping its economy of innovation and excellence. Such a degradation is the inevitable next act of a socialist victory.

This is because in a socialist system, there are no incentives, only bureaucratic directives that ignore the system's non-performance. Hence the old joke about the Soviet Union, that the authorities pretend to pay wages, and the workers pretend to work. Not surprisingly, when Lenin and Mao centralized control of agriculture ostensibly to make the production and distribution of food fairer, the result in both countries was starvation that killed tens of millions of people. Venezuela's management of the economy, meant to provide for all equally, emptied store shelves (admittedly, a kind of equality, although the elites now have their own well-stocked stores).

Such attempts to raze the supply-side of the economy blaze a fast trail to socialism. If incentives for producers and workers do not matter, then neither can a government takeover of "the means of production"—either by predatory taxes or outright confiscation. Socialist economists insist you can have socialism without suffering any downsides. In Venezuela, the confiscation of businesses by Hugo Chávez, elected to implement a socialist agenda, led the economy to collapse. Hyperinflation ensued. When Nicolás Maduro succeeded Chávez, he attributed prices to "parasites of the bourgeoise."[7] His remedy? Send soldiers into stores to slap new price stickers over goods. The predictable result were shortages, mass starvation, and 4.6 million hungry citizens fleeing the country.[8]

One doesn't have to look to such extremes to see the deficiencies of socialism. In the mildly socialist Nordic countries today, where business is now allowed to flourish, living standards are 15 percent below those of the United States.[9] It seems that these countries, however, are catching on. OECD measures show that in some ways, Nordic countries now have less regulation than the United States.[10] Tax rates on businesses have trended downward. Health care is no longer "free" but requires substantial cost-sharing. Nordic countries tax capital less and regulate product markets less than the United States. The American socialists tout Nordic models that Nordic countries gave up long ago. These countries are becoming social democracies but not socialist countries. Clearly, they've learned something from experience.

While the Nordic countries shift back toward capitalism, the United States is drifting ever leftward. In the Democratic Party, Senator Elizabeth Warren introduced the Accountable Capitalism Act in preparation for her unsuccessful run for the presidency.[11] She would subject any corporation with more than $1 billion in revenue to charter itself as a "United States corporation." This would take us back to the colonial era, when large companies had royal charters like the British East India Company. Under Senator Warren's proposed legislation, chartered "United States corporations" would have to have at least 40 percent of their board members selected by employees, a state-ordered disenfranchisement of the role of the owners—the shareholders, which include millions of pensioners—and confiscation of their property.

Democrats today are also in favor of Medicare for All, which would bring exactly one customer to the health-care counter—the government—who would determine the total revenue that health care providers receive. This would effectively end supply and demand and socialize medicine. If the Democrats succeed, government will control the means of production as surely as in Maduro's Venezuela.

Such a socialist system would degrade the future. It would do so by leaving little incentive for invention and innovation. Who is going to work to invent a new product that someone else will own and give away for free? The answer is obvious when you think of all the life-changing inventions of the last sixty-five years from America's free market, from color television to the cellphone to anti-lock brakes to the personal computer to GPS to the voice-activated personal digital assistant. Can you think of anything comparable invented by a socialist country anywhere at any time that you would actually want? And yet in the United States, many U.S. politicians continue to advocate for greater government control of the economy as being, somehow, "progressive."

The regressive nature of progressive politics is not a matter of opinion. Stanford University economist Edward P. Lazear combined the Fraser Institute's database with income data taken from over 160 countries.[12] What did he find? That socialism degrades the incomes of people, even the poor. Lazear even found a correlation with poverty for countries that included the word "socialist" in their formal name. Conversely, a national move away from socialism raises income, including the poor. "Changing freedom from the Mexico level [with heavy state control and interference] to the Singapore level [largely free market] is predicted to raise the income of the poor by about 40 percent."[13]

Ignoring history and current events, Senator Elizabeth Warren proposes control of capital, with higher tax rates and extensive government control of banks, and with levels of taxation that are confiscatory. Some of her proposals sound eminently reasonable, such as a 3 percent "billionaires' tax" that would only take 3 cents for every dollar earned, and a 2 percent tax on those with a net worth between $50 and $1 billion. Surely Jeff Bezos and Warren Buffett can sustain a little nick like that, right?

But consider: A return on interest rates, unlike investment capital, is risk free. If there is a 2–3 percent tax on wealth and the interest rate is 2 percent, then the risk-free income generated from wealth would be zero. If the rate is raised to 6 percent, as some are now proposing, holding money would often be a negative proposition.

U.S. socialists like Bernie Sanders continue to pine for the remaking of America in the image of '70s-style Nordic socialism, which they hold out as a moderate form of "democratic" socialism. At CEA we ran the numbers on what would happen if the United States aligned our policies with those of the Nordic countries in the 1970s, as Senator Sanders would like. We estimated that if the United States were to adopt these old policies, our economy would eventually shrink by 19 percent. That would amount to a loss of about $11,000 for every person, every year.

And what would happen if the United States adopted the highly socialist policies of Venezuela? When we plugged in the numbers at CEA, we found it would reduce our nation's total wealth by at least 40 percent over the long run, costing each person $24,000 a year.[14]

But it's not just about material well-being. Winston Churchill believed that socialism wasn't just dysfunctional, but evil. And as the roots of American socialism deepen, it has begun to stretch its muscles and indulge its authoritarian impulse. You can see this in the informal authoritarianism of cancel culture, in which a youthful mistake or poorly worded statement leads to a brutal crushing of all prospects. You can see it in elaborate speech codes under which the use of the wrong pronoun makes one a target for harassment. In 2017, mobs prevented speakers from being heard at Claremont McKenna College, Middlebury, the University of Chicago, U.C.–Berkeley, U.C.–Davis, and the University of Washington. It not unusual for conservative speakers to be "milk-shaked" or physically assaulted.

And in the Obama administration, there were apparently no qualms about using the IRS to single out conservative and libertarian organizations for harassment. Democrats today yearn to kill the filibuster, and President Biden has even appointed a commission to study the idea of packing the U.S. Supreme Court.

Democrats are heading down a path that, at its extreme, has been implemented by dictators in Central and South America. They show that a regime can quash democracy in a perfectly "lawful" manner. A skein of laws can be enacted that give government an infinite range of negative incentives that can be wielded to punish dissent—all legally. This is what scholars mean when they speak of replacing "the rule of law" with the "rule by law." Thus the Obama administration was able to abuse the powers of the IRS legally to persecute conservative organizations shorn of any veneer of political neutrality. When the Obama Treasury Department issued a "Be on the Lookout" for tax-exempt organizations, it included labels of conservative organizations.[15]

Far from being more democratic, the very nature of socialism impels it to be anti-democratic, even cruel. The radicalism on display this year suggests that the control of respectability and the media and censorship and canceling on the internet are allowing Democrats to lead us to the end of capitalism. Trump the great disruptor may, ironically, have taught the Left the lessons socialism needed to win once and for all.

\* \* \*

If you are like most Americans, you feel a little bit dazed by the chaotic and conflict-riven four years of the Trump administration. With direct and unfiltered communications, Donald Trump developed a platform from which he could call out his critics. And call them out he did. The ruder he got, the more attention he got, which aroused deep passions in the 74 million Americans who voted for his reelection hoping to continue to try to make America great again. But he also aroused passionate, visceral opposition in his Democratic opponents, whose behavior violated all previously established norms, from planting the Steele Dossier, to threatening to impeach him from his first day in office, to actually impeaching him twice, even after he was gone and defeated. This vehemence cries out for an explanation.

The deeply rooted hatred of Trump on the left wasn't just a question of Trump's manners. Think about it. The Left cried out for social justice, and Donald Trump responded: You want social justice? I'll give you social justice. The president would press me for economic statistics for his tweets, and I can assure you he had excellent material to work with. In many ways, 2018 and 2019 were the best years for economic measures of social justice in American history.

Over Donald Trump's first three years in office, 6.6 million people were lifted out of poverty, the largest reduction in poverty since the "War on Poverty" began. Real median income increased 6.8 percent in 2019, the largest increase on record. Real median income for African Americans saw a bigger increase in a single year than was experienced during the entire eight years of the Obama administration.[16] Income inequality increased under President Obama and declined under President Trump.

Trump received no credit for these advances. If anything, his successes made his opponents even more crazed. It is clear to me now that

Donald Trump found himself in the middle of a much bigger historical battle than the simple fight against Joe Biden or Hillary Clinton. He came to power determined to arrest and reverse the Drift to socialism. The entire Donald Trump saga only makes sense if one views him as powerful opposition to the Left's quest to defeat capitalism and turn the United States into a socialist country. To understand Donald Trump and where we go from here, we have to get back to Joseph Schumpeter.

★ ★ ★

A refugee academic from Vienna, Schumpeter was an admirer of capitalism who did not believe that capitalism could survive. Writing almost a century ago, he predicted a time when the Left would defeat capitalism once and for all. Schumpeter's writings point to five factors that would eventually destroy capitalism which, in honor of Schumpeter's famously brilliant horsemanship, I'll call the Five Horsemen of the Apocalypse. Schumpeter traced the Drift from its headwaters and followed its natural course, allowing him to predict today's ascendant Left with perfect clarity.

## The First Horseman: Intellectuals

The first horseman is the entrenched hostility to capitalism by intellectuals. Schumpeter recognized that professors aren't the only intellectuals. The term also includes people who we identify today as journalists and various kinds of literary, television, cinematic, and online thought leaders.

"Intellectuals are in fact people who wield the power of the spoken and the written word," Schumpeter said. Then he made an acerbic observation that one of the features "that distinguish [intellectuals] from other people who do the same is the absence of direct responsibility for practical affairs."[17] They serve, he wrote, as "the intellectual spectator."[18] They are not practitioners with intellectual tools or talent, like brain surgeons or SpaceX engineers. They are professional talkers and thinkers, people the ancient Greeks would have called "sophists."

Why do intellectuals cling to anti-capitalism? To the intellectual, "indignation about the wrongs of capitalism simply represents the logical inference from outrageous facts."[19] Schumpeter saw the intellectuals' faith in socialism as a sort of passion, likening it to a lover's blind belief that his infatuation represents something noble in his beloved. No matter how many lives are ruined by terrible public schools in urban areas, opposition to charter schools must be maintained. No matter how many states and administrations demonstrate that high taxes injure growth and family incomes, high taxes must never be questioned.

Conservatives like to say that "ideas have consequences." True enough. But Schumpeter understood that ideas alone won't bring about change because he saw a feedback loop between ideas and culture, which maintains a general hostility toward capitalism. If you doubt this, consider: When was the last time you saw a movie in which a corporation was anything but a villain?

Think here of Michael Moore, the documentary director, or Rachel Maddow, the commentator on MSNBC. They are intellectuals, sure, but they draw their energy from mixing it up with activist, left-wing allies. They have their feet on the ground next to the organizers, activists, and grassroots of the Left.

Such intellectuals aren't the cause of anti-capitalism, but they know how to dramatize and articulate it. "The role of the intellectual group consists primarily in stimulating, energizing, verbalizing and organizing this material and only secondarily in adding to it," Schumpeter wrote.[20]

Frustration with democracy is an understandable impulse. Such intellectuals of the Left—and growing numbers on the right—are so impatient with the slow, herky-jerky progress of democracy that they are ready to degrade democracy, if not discard it altogether.

Democracy sometimes feels like the Greek myth of Sisyphus. In the myth, Zeus punishes Sisyphus for cheating death and returning to the world from Hades. The condemned man's punishment is to work a boulder up a hill forever. Each time Sisyphus labors almost to the top, the boulder tumbles back down, forcing him to start all over again. Democracy can remind one of that task of endlessly pushing the boulder up the hill. It is easy to overlook that at times, however, boulders do get to the top, as when Lyndon Johnson signed the Civil Rights Act of 1964, Ronald Reagan signed the Kemp–Roth tax cuts of 1981, Barack Obama used a Democratic majority to pass the Affordable Care Act in 2010, and Donald Trump signed into law his Tax Cuts and Jobs Act in 2017 and used constitutional means to reshape the judiciary. Even if democracy at times feels like a sorry, futile labor, it's as good as it's going to get for mere mortals.

It is not just Democrats and progressives who are so frustrated with the norms of capitalism and a democratic republic that they would discard the rules. Some Republicans want socialism too; they just want it in a right-wing form instead of a left-wing one. Senator Josh Hawley has proposed a "Trust-Busting for the Twenty-First Century Act," which would amount to a sweepingly socialist takeover of capitalism.[21] Senator Hawley would ban mergers and acquisitions for firms with a market cap of over $100 billion. He sells his proposal as a corrective to the censorship of Big Tech firms like Facebook, Twitter, and Google, but his bill would subject about eighty U.S. corporations to a rule that would calcify capitalism. He would lower the threshold for prosecution under existing federal antitrust laws. And just in case business still didn't get the point, Hawley would expand the power of the Federal Trade Commission and require any company that loses federal antitrust lawsuits to "forfeit all their profits resulting from monopolistic conduct."[22] Under such subjective standards, the latter could easily amount to a corporate death penalty.

Some conservatives are taking Donald Trump's corrective, populist shift of Republicans' focus from big business to workers, to an anti-capitalist extreme that embraces the Democratic-socialist philosophy of "rule by law"—with so many ways for regulators to punish corporations that executives would have to vet every business decision with Biden's regulators in Washington. The result, ironically, would be corporations that get even more "woke" and workers who are worse off.

While politicians make proposals, intellectuals flesh out the indictment of capitalism, give it intellectual respectability and policy goals to promote. They help radicalize politics. So who generates the anti-capitalism?

## The Second Horseman: The University

Higher education molds the left-wing intellectual and bestows his or her credentials. Writing in the 1930s, Schumpeter foresaw that higher education would increase in importance and size as capitalism deepened. It would expand to educate the growing population of white-collar workers. But the growth rate of higher education would soon exceed the growth rate of knowledge-intensive, white-collar jobs. The result would be, in Schumpeter's words, a "particularly important case of sectional unemployment."[23]

The glut of graduates from universities, Schumpeter wrote, would likely drive their wages below those of manual blue-collar labor. Think of all the exquisitely well-educated people you know who make less money than the manager of a Starbucks. But Schumpeter saw that the college graduate is usually repelled by manual occupations, though unable to do professional work like accounting or serving as a dental assistant.

So the intellectuals drift . . . to become "intellectual spectators." They cohere into an interest group centered around the educational system that produced them. They come to control the university's greatest power, the university's ability to confer or deny credentials, an immense but underestimated power: the power to grant, withhold, or rescind respectability. And armed with this power, the intellectuals inculcate a general hostility to capitalism among their students.

Before conceding to Joe Biden in the early throes of the coronavirus pandemic, Bernie Sanders drew support from about one-half of American college students. And why should he not be popular? He sounds like every student's professor, running on a platform aligned with the utopian socialist ideals presented every day by faculty. Bernie promised to create a single payer national healthcare system, advocated a Green New Deal amounting to a Venezuela-style government takeover of the energy sector, free college for all, double the proportion of Americans in unions, and government provision of government-owned housing.[24]

A 2019 College Pulse poll found that 39 percent of college students held a "very favorable" or "somewhat favorable" view of socialism. One College Pulse poll showed that for humanities majors, the favorable view of socialism was even higher, including almost 80 percent of philosophy majors. Approximately 58 percent of English and international relations majors held "very favorable" or "somewhat favorable" views of socialism.[25]

As Schumpeter predicted, higher education has evolved to the point where a defense of free markets is an extraordinary act of bravery for a student or a young professor trying to earn tenure.

But don't think that highly educated socialists are happy campers. Given that tenure-tracked, academic jobs are scarce, there are many failed would-be academics bitter about their fate. Meanwhile, the depressed wages of those who do become professors instill a secret sense of inferiority, something guaranteed to promote anger. Those who go into journalism, unless they reach the very top of the profession or have a trust fund, accept a career track in a business that has been wrecked and pulled apart by social media.

So who is held responsible for the plight of the underemployed academic and journalist? It must be capitalism. There must be something morally wrong in a society where brilliant scholars are paid far less than the guy who owns five ice cream parlors in the suburbs.

A survey of Harvard faculty found that 1.46 percent identified as "conservative" or "very conservative," while about 80 percent identified as "liberal." And Harvard is hardly an outlier in this respect. Of 2,081 political donations by college professors in 31 states and the District of Columbia in 2020, only 22 went to Republicans. Between 1940 and

2015, the share of Americans with bachelor's degrees roughly tripled. So did the extent of Americans' indoctrination by the Left.[26]

## The Third Horseman: How Capitalism Weakens Religion

Schumpeter would not agree with Karl Marx's characterization of religion as "the sigh of the oppressed creature."[27] But he recognized that capitalism set the stage for socialism's rejection of religion. In the Renaissance, early capitalism—the first stock markets, banks, and water-powered mills—emerged out of a new spirit of calculation and ingenuity. Capitalism's pragmatic, worldly way of thinking wrought economic miracles but at the expense of extinguishing the spirit of the Middle Ages with its mystic, humble view of God and authority.

"The capitalist process rationalizes behavior and ideas and by so doing chases from our minds, along with metaphysical belief, mystic and romantic ideals of all sorts," Schumpeter wrote.[28]

Capitalism is a bazaar that draw us into secular activities throughout the day. It narcotizes us at night. As we move through our day from our Zoom calls and emails, buying something from Amazon, purchasing stocks online through E*Trade, watching a new blockbuster on Netflix, the suggestion of taking time for the sacred, to read holy scripture or pray seems quaint and antiquated. Who has the time for that?

Capitalism, with a practical spirit that is rational and anti-heroic, does not kill religion outright. It crowds it out with responsibilities, entertainment, and other distractions.

Yet this tendency of capitalism to smother religion still leaves a void within the human psyche, the niche once occupied by religion. Human beings want to experience beauty, grandeur, awe, and purpose. It is this hunger for something transcendent that leads so many to religion. High art, Schumpeter says, can sometimes fill this "extrarational" niche, satisfying cravings previously addressed by religion. In our day, this niche can be filled partly by the latest showing of David Hockney paintings, or by popular entertainments, whether streaming television or *Grand Theft Auto V*.

But for most people, art and entertainment cannot fill the void for long. The hollowing of religion by capitalism creates a craving for transcendence that socialism can exploit. For it is socialism, Schumpeter argues, that can meet our hunger for something sacred, for the transformative and transcendent.

Like a religion, Marxism offers a "system of ultimate ends" that can give meaning to one's life, "absolute standards by which to judge events and actions."[29] And, he wrote, Marxism "implies a plan of salvation and the indication of the evil from which mankind, or a chosen section of mankind, is to be saved." It promises "paradise on this side of the grave."[30]

Even the supposedly religious are making a religion of wokeness. The leadership of the Episcopal church has called for "net neutrality," higher taxes on the rich, heightened regulation of banks, and a higher minimum wage.[31] It seems oblivious to the fact that Christ never preached about net neutrality or a higher minimum wage. He did constantly remind us that we have a responsibility to help the poorest among us. But when did Christ ever preach that we should raise the minimum wage with the earnings of the owner of a small hamburger franchise who operates on a thin margin?

If you believe Marx was not wrong to call religion "the opiate of the masses," then socialism in the twenty-first century is our fentanyl: the modern, synthetic, more lethal successor to opium.

## The Fourth Horseman: The Campaign against the Nuclear Family

Economic textbooks portray people as self-interested, rational actors, as if we were a nation of emotionless Mr. Spocks. In real economic life, many critical decisions made by workers and consumers spring not from pure selfishness, but from intergenerational concerns about the family and future generations.

This "family motive" is noble. It draws us out of ourselves, Schumpeter wrote, by making us think not just of the long-term wellbeing of our inheritance, but of the kind of world our children and grandchildren will live in. It is the stuff of all our hopes and dreams.

Even the desire to have a family, in Schumpeter's view, prompts us to save, invest, and to try to excel. As capitalism arose, people shifted from consumption of farm-fueled subsistence diets to the accumulation of wealth. In seventeenth century Europe, capitalism emerged at least in part as the result of a struggle for property rights to ensure that one's wealth would persist for future generations.

But the dwindling of the nuclear family today brings us back to short-term thinking and selfish consumption. Look at the declining fortunes of parts of Europe today as fertility rates fall below the population's replacement rate in many countries, plunging whole towns and villages into vacancy. It seems to me that the loss of family leaves many singletons caught in a kind of shallow hedonism that is ultimately nihilistic.

One thing Schumpeter did not foresee was that in modern socialism, opposition to capitalism would be combined with opposition to the nuclear family. The website of Black Lives Matter posted (until it was noted in the media and deleted): "We disrupt the Western-prescribed nuclear family structure requirement by supporting each other as extended families and 'villages' that collectively care for one another, especially our children. . . ."[32]

This hostility to the traditional family was what former Vice President Dan Quayle was getting at years ago when he questioned the social impact of an episode of *Murphy Brown* that celebrated single motherhood by a rich woman. For people who are not wealthy like the fictional Murphy Brown, raising a child alone can be a daunting and lonely prospect. There are few things as clear in social science as the correlation between what used to be called "a broken home" and the likelihood a child will drop out of school, take drugs, or get involved in crime and be poor for life.[33] Quayle was ridiculed, but the birth rate among single women since the Murphy Brown era has increased dramatically.[34]

# The Fifth Horseman: The Corporation against Itself

As capitalism made America richer, it has created wealth for people to live well, in many cases very well, off of high professional salaries and returns on their capital investments. This has the effect of cutting off capitalists from the practice and culture of capitalism as more and more people get rich without taking risks in new ventures.

Many succeed as managers and administrators, as in-house counsels, accountants, and IT managers. Within this hierarchy, the internal corporate processes these professionals manage become ever more layered and complex. And thus the structure and culture of corporations "unavoidably acquire the characteristics of a bureaucracy," Schumpeter wrote. "Socialism of a very sober type would almost automatically come into being."[35]

Simply put, capitalists lose touch with capitalism. Foundations set up by arch-capitalists like Henry Ford or John D. Rockefeller become dependable funders of radical, left-wing causes. Corporations themselves are actively pursuing social justice rather than profit maximization. Michael Bloomberg makes billions of dollars from capitalism, governed New York City well as a law-and-order mayor, but also spends hundreds of millions of dollars on left-wing causes and political campaigns.

As pressure from progressives grows, many corporations make a conscious calculation. Because Republicans believe in free markets, low taxes, low regulation, and the rule of law, they see little price to pay in offending Republicans. But progressives are more than willing to use powerful defamation and cultural and political pressure-tactics to humiliate and injure corporations. This explains why so many companies, from Coca-Cola to Delta Airlines to Nike, are suddenly so "woke." A 2019 study by the prestigious National Bureau of Economic Research found that most CEO donations are to Republicans. But corporations tend to publicize their donations to left-wing causes and are reticent to acknowledge those to conservative causes.[36] The best explanation for that pattern is that companies fear retribution from Democrats but not from Republicans. Thus, in the aftermath of the passage of the Georgia election law, several big corporations lined up with Democrats against Republicans in the belief that this was a good insurance policy, with no price to pay.

These many ironies are the result of a natural evolution.

Think of successful liberals you know. Many are, in the strictest sense, still capitalists, owning stock shares and bonds. But they are far removed from the capitalism of the entrepreneur. By the time this metamorphosis is complete, the other four horsemen will have arrived on the scene.

The first horseman creates a class of intellectuals shaped by socialism who have become its stoutest defenders. Their ranks are swelled by the preponderance of higher education, which churns out left-wing youth with the efficiency with which the U.S. Mint spits out new coins. These intellectuals discredit the family, driving social dysfunctions that capitalist society seems unable to deal with. They've found that if you control the elite universities, pretty soon you will control the corporate media.

A past study found that 100 percent—100 percent!—of political donations by CBS news employees went to Democrats.[37] Other networks were almost as tilted. Another study by professors at the University of Virginia, Florida State, and Brigham Young University found that the typical journalist on Twitter is far to the left of Barack Obama or even the median Senate Democrat. In fact, the study indicates that journalists on Twitter most frequently fall between Bernie Sanders and Alexandria Ocasio-Cortez in terms of their ideological preferences.[38] The scholars at these three institutions found that Republican presidents receive between 20 and 30 percent less positive coverage in all newspapers than Democratic presidents, and up to 40 percent less positive coverage by the top ten newspapers.[39]

I experienced the slant against a Republican president firsthand. Good economic news under President Trump, such as record employment of women and African Americans, or a more than $6,000 increase in real income for Americans, would have been extolled in rapturous terms if Obama had still been president. Many news outlets, controlled by cowed corporations, never even reported these facts under President Trump.

And the media will strive to make it so disreputable to stand up to the politically correct socialist dogma inculcated at universities that capitalism will die, Schumpeter believed, because nobody will be courageous enough to stand up to a hostile media's withering scorn and defend it.

The middle and upper-middle class will give up on defending capitalism. They will be meek, Schumpeter wrote, because "the bourgeois order no longer makes any sense to the bourgeoisie itself and that, when all is said and nothing is done, it does not really care."[40] Hillary Clinton famously spent a fortune preparing her victory party, renting the giant Javits Center in New York City and arranging for fireworks to be shot off over the Hudson. President Trump was so uncertain of his victory that, at the last minute, Jared Kushner had to find a place to hold a victory party as it became increasingly clear that Trump might win. Everyone thought Trump would lose to Clinton because the media told them so. Clinton was so confident because she, without reference to the original, had supreme faith in Schumpeter's vision.

## CHAPTER ELEVEN

# The Way Forward

In July 1945, Winston Churchill faced the voters having rallied the free world against Nazi Germany to win one of the most improbable victories in history. In 1939, it was hard for most Britons to imagine their country surviving an onslaught from the ruthless empire just across the English Channel. Churchill persuaded his countrymen that they could not only survive but ultimately achieve victory. When victory came in May 1945, it made him a national hero like none other. So in facing the socialist Labour Party and its leader, Clement Attlee, in a general election, Churchill confidently went on the offensive. He took to the airwaves of the BBC to define his openly socialist opponents as enemies of freedom.

Against the advice of his advisors and wife, Clementine, Churchill spoke in blunt, even brutal, terms:

> Socialism is inseparably interwoven with Totalitarianism and the abject worship of the State. . . . There is to be one State to which all are to be obedient in every act of their lives. This State is to be arch-employer, the arch-planner, the arch-administrator and ruler, and the arch-caucus boss. . . . Socialism is, in its

essence, an attack not only upon British enterprise, but upon the right of the ordinary man or woman to breathe freely without having a harsh, clumsy, tyrannical hand clapped across their mouths and nostrils.[1]

Churchill was heavily influenced by Friedrich Hayek, author of the 1944 bestseller *The Road to Serfdom*. Hayek titled one chapter "Why the Worst Get on Top." Hayek wrote, "It is then the man or party who seems strong enough to 'get things done' who exercises the greatest appeal."[2] The worst people and impulses rise when moderate Democrats and socialists are frustrated by the Sisyphean task of rolling boulders up hills. This is the point that the Biden Democrats are at now. They are ready to throw out the existing order, to turn the Senate into a simple, majoritarian body like the House, or get rid of it altogether, pack the Supreme Court with progressive jurists, and turn a portion of an urban area called Washington, D.C., into a state. Such radical revisions of the American constitutional order are necessary in order to enact socialism.

As a party becomes more dedicated to enacting socialism, it necessarily becomes more totalitarian and less accepting of pluralism and debate. "What they will seek is somebody with such solid support as to inspire confidence that he can carry out whatever he wants," Hayek wrote. "It is here that the new type of party, organized on military lines, comes in."[3]

At the end of the 1945 campaign, Churchill tried to expand on such warnings about socialism before a large crowd at a greyhound racing track in East London, only to be booed down by a large contingent of Labour rowdies. Churchill complained he had trouble being heard over the "booing party." But that booing party drowned him out. Churchill's Conservative Party majority collapsed in the general election. He would not have the chance to return as prime minister until the 1950s.[4]

How could such a great leader lose an election months after saving the country?

Churchill had misjudged the moment. After years of sacrifice and privation, the war-exhausted British people were ready to elect the party that promised to raid the rich in order to dole out "free" health care, housing, and benefits.

This history lesson contains both a warning and an opportunity for us in the Biden era.

The American people have not come out of a major war. But the economic ravages of the pandemic, coupled with diminished prospects for Millennials trying to establish solid careers, have left many Americans exhausted and susceptible to socialism's siren song. Like Attlee, Joe Biden is too mild-mannered and practical to seem like the enabler of radicalism that he is. But, like Attlee, Biden has the potential to be stampeded by his more radical supporters into running the country deep into socialism, and to do so with considerable public support.

Comparing the defeats of 1945 and 2020, however, also yields a happy realization: *Clearly, voters in many developed democracies are learning to be wary of socialism.*

Winston Churchill's Conservatives were trounced, losing 189 seats. Donald Trump may have lost his bid for re-election, but he won 74 million votes—more than any candidate in history after Biden. A shift of 45,000 votes would have put him at the threshold of victory. While Biden ran as a centrist and defeated the openly socialist Bernie Sanders, it soon became clear to voters that the radical firebrand, Brooklyn barista Congresswoman Alexandria Ocasio-Cortez and her progressive allies were setting the Democratic agenda of defunding the police, raising taxes, socializing American industry through a "Green New Deal," Medicare for All, and enforcing speech codes on ordinary Americans. With the selection of the most "progressive" member of the United States Senate, Kamala Harris, as the seventy-eight-year-old Biden's running mate, it became clear to voters that the socialist tail will always wag the dog in a Biden administration.[5]

But the improvement of modern Republicans (and British Tories) in the race against socialism shows that it is possible to win, or at least compete, against socialism.

Trump, after all, overcame such overwhelming odds in 2016 and almost again in 2020. How did he do it? It clearly was not the result of a detailed master plan. I would wager that President Trump doesn't sit up at night reading Schumpeter. But from the start he has shown an instinctive understanding of the dangers of socialism and the nature of the forces propelling it along within the universities, the media, and the Swamp. And the Left's control over "respectability" had no pull on him. He took pleasure in goading them to distraction.

I would wager as well that Donald Trump has never read media theorist and philosopher Marshall McLuhan. But the former president has lived out the decades-old insight of McLuhan, seeing a way around the intellectual and media cartel that Schumpeter expected would defeat capitalism once and for all.

In the 1960s, McLuhan looked ahead to the wired world and anticipated its impact on humanity with a clarity matching Schumpeter's. He offered a framework for how social media would work decades before Trump tweeted his way into the White House.

McLuhan understood that the medium through which we consume information shapes society and our individual experiences of life. "All media work us over completely. They are so pervasive in their personal, political, economic, aesthetic, psychological, moral, ethical, and social consequences that they leave no part of us untouched, unaffected, unaltered," he wrote, before famously concluding: "The medium is the message."[6]

McLuhan also said, "TV tends to foster patterns rather than events."[7] In other words, TV provides a narrative with a theme and a moral. He foresaw that viewers of Rachel Maddow on MSNBC or Chris Cuomo on CNN hear more than mere descriptions of events. Those viewers soak in Rachel's or Chris's morality tales.

Anticipating something much like the internet, McLuhan foresaw the emergence of a "global village" that would unite people in Japan,

South Africa, Argentina, and the United States in following a common story, whether that be the drama of rescuers' trying to reach a child stuck in a well, a policeman pressing his knee on the neck of a man before a crowd pleading for his life, or *Tiger King* and what really happened to Carole Baskin's husband.[8] Gone are the days when TV evening news and the daily newspaper curated our information. McLuhan realized we would personalize our own news feeds. With Twitter especially, but also with YouTube and Facebook, society is reverting to its visual and oral origins.

In the 1990s, magazines and books waxed in rhapsodic prose about how the internet would bring us all together. McLuhan earlier realized that the new media would instead "retribalize" society. Thirty years prior, McLuhan foresaw the nastiness of the internet when "electronic man wears his brain outside of his skull and his nervous system on top of his skin. Such a creature is ill tempered. . . . Loss of individualism invites once again the comfort of tribal loyalties."[9]

It is hard to believe these words were written more than half-a-century ago.

Later, in a television interview, McLuhan dug deeper into the impact that these new technologies would have on individuals, "You see the circuit doesn't simply push things out for inspection, it pushes you into the circuit, it involves you."[10] The new technology would destroy "what is left of personal privacy . . . politically destabilizing entire nations."[11]

That must have sounded abstract, far-fetched, even science-fictional, when McLuhan uttered those words. Now, his words ring true.

Trump instinctively understood all of this. Before Twitter banned him, he had accumulated more followers of @realDonaldTrump than there were American households tuning in to the most-watched television show of the 1960s. He strategically used outlandish and even outrageous tactics to attract attention, expand his audience, and discredit a hostile media. In 2017, for instance, the most retweeted tweet from the president was a vintage video of Donald Trump punching an opponent at Wrestlemania, with the opponent's head replaced with a CNN bobblehead.[12] In

2019, he posted a photograph of his head over that of Rocky Balboa. During the election, Trump posted a doctored clip of Joe and Hunter Biden in a Nickelback music video.

For better or worse, Trump's campaign proved how the world has been changed by an unprecedented competition for attention. Trump grasped that the power of Twitter could be weaponized against "fake news" and "the Swamp." It could be used to stave off the opponents of capitalism—for now.

Schumpeter's dark vision did not include anything like Twitter, a world in which politicians could appeal directly to voters and organize them. It is impossible to imagine the success of Donald Trump without his rallies and Twitter. Social media gave Trump a powerful new way to sidestep the culture curators and their media filters, to communicate with individual voters, and for many of them to communicate with him and each other.

Other politicians have used Twitter. But President Trump used Twitter to such devastating effect on the mainstream media by posting constantly. It was not uncommon for the president to post dozens of tweets every day. He habituated his followers to look for the next "treat," while attracting more followers by his willingness to be shocking.

Barack Obama, ever the organizer, primarily used social media to mobilize supporters as a mass and raise money from large numbers of small donors. Trump spoke to the ambitions, hopes, fears, and resentments of individuals.

Previous presidents had struggled to refute the prevailing narrative and defy the consensus. Only candidate and President Trump was effective in calling BS on that consensus, branding it "fake news." His campaign rhetoric drew the wrath of the bipartisan establishment, but his instincts were more accurate than the models used by the Ph.D. crowd or the media's narratives.

He offered hope to people who saw the Left's assault on their religion, their nuclear family, and their capitalist system. He promised fairer, "America-first" policies on trade, tariffs, regulations, and job creation.

Republicans might wish for a polite, "civilized" candidate who would espouse pro-capitalist policies, but that wish is a denial of the evolution of our society. Trump won the competition for attention on the internet by being outrageous. Absent his brazen behavior, the Left's control of polite society and the media would have likely doomed any other Republican to defeat.

An important analysis of Trump's 2016 victory was published in the *Harvard Business Review* just after his election. The article lead with the punchline: "While no hard proof exists that his tweets put him over the top in the election, they undeniably riveted the attention of a broad public, media included."[13] The article suggested that Trump proved the advantages of "big seed marketing" whereby a person with the ability to seed messages to many individuals can create a tidal wave of attention. Echoing the observations of McLuhan, who stressed the desire of the spectator to become involved in the content, the analysis continued, "unlike former president Barack Obama, who primarily used social media to mobilize supporters en masse, Trump uses Twitter to address his audience directly as individuals." And herein lies the key. "This seemingly person-to-person disclosure of the man, warts and all, grants coveted authenticity and a stronger base of influence (and backlash) than mass communication ever could."[14] Despite spending almost nothing on television advertising during the primaries, Trump won because of all the free media the controversies he ignited bought. "Traditional media would not have been so complicit if Trump's tweets hadn't been so provocative as to be irresistible," the article concluded. Addictive even, you might say.

The competition for attention has emerged as the kryptonite for the Left's control of American politics. As this becomes more apparent, the Left will continue to turn to the power of inattention, or what we today call "cancel culture." The backlash has been all but complete, with Trump's Twitter account shut down, the competitor of Facebook, Parler, shut down for months and marginalized as well, while conservative books and movies are censored from media and major social media platforms like Amazon books. Snopes.com, which purports to be a neutral fact-checker, has a long-running feud with the conservative humor outlet The Babylon Bee, often analyzing its satire as news reporting. Google threatened to cut the conservative news outlet The Federalist from advertising on its platform.[15] This would have denied The Federalist access to 90 percent of online searches, isolating it from readers and demonetizing it. When challenged by Senator Ted Cruz, Google said it acted not because of any content in The Federalist, but because of the content of its comments section. Senator Cruz pointed out to Google that, as the parent company of YouTube, Google itself hosts many comment sections that are, suffice it to say, not content you'd be proud to associate with.

So Trump's victory in 2016 used new technology to overturn Schumpeter's pessimistic predictions. But was it just a delay of the inevitable?

Perhaps. Perhaps not.

Many are catching on to what is really going on.

American business is beginning to. There are those like Coca-Cola, Delta Airlines, and Nike that spend shareholder money on social causes unrelated to their core business. But many companies refuse to follow this path. They still seek to invest to maximize profits and participate in politics to the extent they can help guide policies in a friendly direction. Such companies in the long run will tend to be healthier and out-compete those who waste money on proving how "woke" they are. Moreover, as Coca-Cola, Delta, and Nike are learning, what's turnabout is fair play. Conservatives are now running ads denouncing these companies for promoting obesity, overpaying CEOs, and stinking of the "stench of forced labor."[16]

Trump may not be the only one who can play the game, and at some point the cancelers will be unable to keep up with those they would seek to censor. Republicans are starting to follow effective leaders like Governor Ron DeSantis of Florida, Senator Tim Scott of South Carolina, and Congresswoman Elise Stefanik of New York, leaders who can win the competition for attention by being every bit as aggressive, even acerbic, as Donald

Trump. Hope also rests with Democrats like Senators Joe Manchin and Kyrsten Sinema, liberals in the tradition of FDR and RFK, who have made it clear they did not sign up for socialism. Perhaps the greatest hope of all rests in minority communities: the Hispanic owner of a body shop in Los Angeles who is tired of the routine harassment of his small business by regulators and the tax man; the black parents in Detroit who've had it with their children going to public union-controlled schools that have underserved minorities for generations; the hard-working Asian student who faces a hard-and-fast quota system in higher education; the Angelenos who are sick of seeing Venice Beach turned into a homeless encampment; and the New Yorkers disgusted to see Washington Park turned into an open-air market for drugs and prostitution.

As progressives enforce their policies across cities and states, Americans are living out the consequences. As a result, subterranean pressure is building among traditional Democrat constituencies that one day will surely explode like a volcano.

One can hope that the more experience Americans have with progressivism and socialism, the more they will turn back to what is right and what works. The fate of America doesn't have to rest in the hands of a distant elite. It comes down to you, whether you admire or hate Donald Trump, whether you're a Republican or a Democrat. If you believe that the system we grew up with, for all its shortcomings and flaws, is morally and practically superior to socialism, you need to become an activist for freedom.

Donald Trump's words in his 2019 State of the Union address resonated with millions. After speaking of the "brutality" that has resulted from the socialist policies of the Maduro regime in Venezuela, the president said, "Here, in the United States, we are alarmed by new calls to adopt socialism in our country. America was founded on liberty and independence—not government coercion, domination, and control. We are born free, and we will stay free."[17]

Then he said, "Tonight, we renew our resolve that America will never be a socialist country."

As social media transforms society and how people relate to one another, it is clear that the contest to control content will decide whether or not capitalism will be able to hold its own against socialism. If the winning ideas of the free market and the shining ideals of America's Founding can find leverage online and maneuver around the cancel culture, we will have a fighting chance. The secret to defending capitalism is for *many* voices to spring up to defend it with the courage that Donald Trump exhibited. That defense is easy as an intellectual matter, since the facts will always be on the side of free markets. The ruling elites may try to bully and intimidate people into staying quiet as the Drift continues, but their defeat is inevitable if enough people recognize the game the socialists are playing and refuse to be bullied into silence. Schumpeter worried that there would be no voices left to defend capitalism. Yours will suffice.

# Acknowledgements

This book is only possible because President Donald Trump entrusted the job of CEA chairman to me at a critical time in our nation's history. I will always be grateful for the opportunity he offered me to serve my country.

I am also grateful to Steven Mnuchin and Gary Cohn for advising the president to choose me. Larry Kudlow kept me sane in the White House, and much of the progress we made pushing back against the Drift in the Trump White House found its intellectual grounding in his work. Absent Larry, and our close friend Art Laffer, the fight might already have been lost. Finally, the CEA often finds itself on the periphery of White House policymaking. From the beginning of my time in the White House, Jared Kushner and Ivanka Trump always made sure I had a seat at the table when it mattered most.

I would like to thank Joe Sullivan and Mark Davis for their assistance in putting this book together, and D. J. Nordquist for all of her support while she acted as my chief of staff at CEA. I would also like to thank Rafe Sagalyn, who has always been my strongest advocate, and the top-notch team at Regnery including Tom Spence and Harry Crocker.

Thanks to Larry Lindsey for inspiring me to think carefully about the ruling class and its relationship to capitalism.

My sons, John and Jamie, have been a constant source of love and support throughout this project, even if they do run up the score against their dad on the basketball court occasionally. Finally, I thank my father, John Hassett, who dedicated his career to teaching high school English students in Greenfield, Massachusetts. I was blessed to be one of his students. He taught me to love to write and to appreciate great writing.

# Notes

Chapter One
The Trump Legacy: Disrupting the Drift toward
Socialism

1. Morgan Gstalter, "7 in 10 Millennials Say They Would Vote for a Socialist:
   Poll," *The Hill*, October 28, 2019, https://thehill.com/homenews/campaign/467
   684-70-percent-of-millennials-say-theyd-vote-for-a-socialist-poll.

2. Geoffrey Pullman, *The Great Eskimo Vocabulary Hoax and Other Irreverant
   Essays on the Study of Language* (Chicago, Illinois: University of Chicago Press,
   1991), 166–69.

3. Joe Weisenthal, "3 Separate Economists Made the Exact Same Joke about Janet
   Yellen Today," *Business Insider*, August 22, 2014, https://www.businessinsider
   .com/yellen-two-handed-economist-joke-2014-8.

4. Christopher Marquis, "Biden's Push for a More Noble Capitalism Is Destined to
   Fail," *The Hill*, April 2, 2021, https://thehill.com/opinion/finance/546198-bi
   dens-push-for-a-more-noble-capitalism-is-destined-to-fail.

5. "Joseph Alois Schumpeter," Encyclopedia Biographies, Library of Economics
   and Liberty, https://www.econlib.org/library/Enc/bios/Schumpeter.html.

6. Jenni Fink, "Is Sen. Rand Paul or Dr. Fauci Right about Gain-of-Function
   Research Funding in Wuhan?" *Newsweek*, July 22, 2021,
   https://www.newsweek.com/sen-rand-paul-dr-fauci-right-about-gain-function-research-
   funding-wuhan-1612371.

7.  Chris Kutarna, "Marshall McLuhan Decodes Our Present," Medium, January 17, 2018, https://medium.com/@christopherkutarna/marshall-mcluhan-decodes -our-present-7a2842490c32.

## Chapter Two
## Trial by Trump

1.  Penny Star, "Donald Trump's Pick for Top Economic Adviser Is Pro-Immigration, Pro-Outsourcing," Breitbart, April 9, 2017, https://www.breitbart .com/politics/2017/04/09/donald-trump-economic-adviser-pro-immigration-pro -outsourcing/.
2.  Kevin Hassett, "Trump's Run for President Requires Memory Loss: Kevin Hassett," Bloomberg, February 21, 2011, https://www.bloomberg.com/news/ar ticles/2011-02-22/trump-run-for-president-requires-memory-loss-commentary -by-kevin-hassett.
3.  Kevin Hassett and Stan A. Veuger, "Deflating 'Deflategate,'" *New York Times*, June 12, 2015, https://www.nytimes.com/2015/06/14/opinion/deflating-deflateg ate.html.
4.  Mitch McConnell, "Time to Stop the Democrats' Obstruction," *Politico*, April 1, 2019, https://www.politico.com/magazine/story/2019/04/01/mitch-mcconnell -obstruction-democrats-226341.
5.  Josh Zumbrun, "Senate Confirms Kevin Hassett as Chairman of President's Council of Economic Advisors," *Wall Street Journal*, June 7, 2017, https://www .wsj.com/articles/senate-to-vote-on-kevin-hassett-as-cea-chairman-1505233836.

## Chapter Three
## Showboats and Human Torpedoes

1.  "There Was No Booing of Ivanka," *Bild*, April 26, 2017, https://www.bild.de/po litik/ausland/ivanka-trump/berlin-visit-there-was-no-booing-for-ivanka-trump -51469066.bild.html.
2.  Simon Lester, Inu Manak, and Kyounghwa Kim, "Trump's First Trade Deal: The Slightly Revised Korea-U.S. Free Trade Agreement," Cato Institute, June 13, 2019, https://www.cato.org/publications/free-trade-bulletin/trumps-first-trade -deal-slightly-revised-korea-us-free-trade.
3.  "Factbox: German Exposure to U.S. Tariffs on European Car Imports," Reuters, February 22, 2019, https://www.reuters.com/article/us-usa-trade-ger many-cars-factbox/factbox-german-exposure-to-u-s-tariffs-on-european-car-im ports-idUSKCN1QB2H1.
4.  C. Textor, "China's Share of Global Gross Domestic Product (GDP) Adjusted for Purchasing-Power-Parity (PPP) from 2010 to 2020 with Forecasts until 2026," Statista, April 7, 2021, https://www.statista.com/statistics/270439/chinas -share-of-global-gross-domestic-product-gdp/.
5.  "Economic Report of the President," Council of Economic Advisers, February 21, 2018, https://www.govinfo.gov/features/ERP-2018.

## Chapter Four
## The Forest and the Trees

1.  Matthew Yglesias, "Donald Trump's Trade Team Has Based Their Analysis on a Remarkably Silly Mistake," Vox, December 21, 2016, https://www.vox.com /2016/12/21/14044376/trump-navarro-ross.
2.  Doug Palmer, "Why Steel Tariffs Failed When Bush Was President," Politico, March 7, 2018, https://www.politico.com/story/2018/03/07/steel-tariffs-trump -bush-391426.
3.  Bloomberg Quicktake (@Quicktake), "Trump: 'Trade Wars Are Good and Easy to Win,'" Twitter, March 2, 2018, https://twitter.com/i/events/96951990609710 6944?lang=en.
4.  Jim Tankersley, "Trump's Washing Machine Tariffs Stung Consumers While Lifting Corporate Profits," New York Times, April 21, 2019, https://www.nyt imes.com/2019/04/21/business/trump-tariffs-washing-machines.html.
5.  Ibid.
6.  "'Estás en Tu Casa', Dice Peña Nieto a Migrantes; Ofrece Trabajo, Salud y Educación a Centroamericanos," La Vanguardia, October 26, 2018, https://van guardia.com.mx/articulo/estas-en-tu-casa-dice-pena-nieto-migrantes-ofrece-tra bajo-salud-y-educacion.
7.  David Folkenflik, "Tensions Rise at Fox News over Coverage and Rhetoric Surrounding Migrant Caravan," NPR, October 30, 2018, https://www.npr.org /2018/10/30/662253600/tensions-rise-at-fox-news-over-coverage-and-rhetoric -surrounding-migrant-caravan.
8.  Adam Serwer, "Trump's Caravan Hysteria Led to This," The Atlantic, October 28, 2018, https://www.theatlantic.com/ideas/archive/2018/10/caravan-lie-spar ked-massacre-american-jews/574213/.
9.  "Trump Adviser Pressed on Costs of Mexico Tariffs," CNN, June 3, 2019, https://www.cnn.com/videos/business/2019/06/03/hassett-mexico-tariffs-costs -to-us-sot-nr.cnn.
10. CBS This Morning, "Bremmer: Trump Threw Starbursts on Table, Told Merkel 'Don't Say I Never Give You Anything,'" YouTube, June 20, 2018, https://www .youtube.com/watch?v=VKjlPty36a8.

## Chapter Five
## Standing Up to China

1.  Veronica Stracqualursi, "10 Times Trump Attacked China and Its Trade Relations with the U.S.," ABC News, November 9, 2017, https://abcnews.go .com/Politics/10-times-trump-attacked-china-trade-relations-us/story?id=4657 2567.
2.  Justin Pierce and Peter Schott, "Trade Liberalization and Mortality: Evidence from U.S. Counties," American Economic Review: Insights 2, no. 1 (March 2020): 47–64, https://pubs.aeaweb.org/doi/pdfplus/10.1257/aeri.20180396.

3. "Opioid Crisis Statistics," About the Epidemic, U.S. Department of Health and Human Services, https://www.hhs.gov/opioids/about-the-epidemic/opioid-crisis-statistics/index.html.
4. Vanda Felbab-Brown, "Fentanyl and Geopolitics: Controlling Opioid Supply from China," Brookings Institution, July 22, 2020, https://www.brookings.edu/research/fentanyl-and-geopolitics-controlling-opioid-supply-from-china/.
5. "U.S. Dependence on China's Rare Earth: Trade War Vulnerability," Aerospace and Defense, Reuters, June 27, 2019, https://www.reuters.com/article/us-usa-trade-china-rareearth-explainer/u-s-dependence-on-chinas-rare-earth-trade-war-vulnerability-idUSKCN1TS3AQ.
6. "2020: Trade in Goods with China," Census.gov, https://www.census.gov/foreign-trade/balance/c5700.html.
7. "Manufacturing in America," Census.gov, October 4, 2019, https://www.census.gov/library/visualizations/2019/comm/manufacturing-in-america-2019.html; "Measuring America: Manufacturing in America: 2016," Census.gov, October 7, 2016, https://www.census.gov/library/visualizations/2016/comm/manufacturing_day2016.html.
8. Ana Swanson and Chris Buckley, "Chinese Solar Companies Tied to Use of Forced Labor," *New York Times*, January 8, 2021, https://www.nytimes.com/2021/01/08/business/economy/china-solar-companies-forced-labor-xinjiang.html.

## Chapter Six
## The Three Percent Promise

1. "Preserving the Industrial History of Franklin County," Museum of Our Industrial Heritage, https://www.visitma.com/business/8929/.
2. Scott A. Hodge, "The Compliance Costs of IRS Regulations," Tax Foundation, June 15, 2016, https://taxfoundation.org/compliance-costs-irs-regulations/.
3. Chris Wellisz, "Prophet of Pessimism," *Finance and Development* 54, no. 2 (June 2017), https://www.imf.org/external/pubs/ft/fandd/2017/06/people.htm.
4. "Economic Report of the President," Council of Economic Advisers, February 2018, https://www.govinfo.gov/content/pkg/ERP-2018/pdf/ERP-2018.pdf.
5. Ibid.
6. Ibid.
7. Michael Smolyansky, Gustavo Suarez, and Alexandra Tabova, "U.S. Corporations' Repatriation of Offshore Profits: Evidence from 2018," Federal Reserve, August 6, 2019, https://www.federalreserve.gov/econres/notes/feds-notes/us-corporations-repatriation-of-offshore-profits-20190806.htm.
8. Jeffrey Anderson, "Economic Growth by President," Hudson Institute, August 8, 2016, https://www.hudson.org/research/12714-economic-growth-by-president.
9. Rick Seltzer, "How Much Are Most Colleges Paying in Endowment Tax," Inside Higher Ed, February 18, 2020, https://www.insidehighered.com/news/2020/02/18/wealthiest-universities-are-paying-big-endowment-tax-bills-how-much-are-others-who.

10. Fareed Zakaria, "Chair of Council of Economic Advisers Defends Tax Math," CNN, October 27, 2017, https://www.cnn.com/videos/tv/2017/10/27/exp-gps-1029-hassett-sot.cnn.

11. Ibid.

12. Lawrence Summers, "Larry Summers: Trump's Budget Is Simply Ludicrous," *Washington Post*, May 23, 2017, https://www.washingtonpost.com/news/wonk/wp/2017/05/23/larry-summers-trumps-budget-is-simply-ludicrous/.

13. Lawrence Summers, "Lawrence Summers: Trump's Top Economist's Tax Analysis Isn't Just Wrong, It's Dishonest," *Washington Post*, October 17, 2017, https://www.washingtonpost.com/news/wonk/wp/2017/10/17/lawrence-summers-trumps-top-economists-tax-analysis-isnt-just-wrong-its-dishonest/.

14. James Nunns, Leonard Burman, Jeffrey Rohaly, and Joseph Rosenberg, "Analysis of Donald Trump's Tax Plan," Tax Policy Center, December 22, 2015, https://www.taxpolicycenter.org/publications/analysis-donald-trumps-tax-plan/full.

15. "A Preliminary Analysis of the Unified Framework," Tax Policy Center, September 27, 2017, https://www.taxpolicycenter.org/publications/preliminary-analysis-unified-framework/full.

16. Howard Gleckman, "Will Corporate Tax Cuts Really Increase Worker Incomes by $4,000?" Tax Policy Center, October 18, 2017, https://www.taxpolicycenter.org/taxvox/will-corporate-tax-cuts-really-increase-worker-incomes-4000.

17. Austan Goolsbee (@Austan_Goolsbee), "Why is Hassett saying this stuff?" Twitter, September 9, 2019, 9:07 a.m., https://twitter.com/Austan_Goolsbee/status/1171047517800325120.

18. Jason Furman (@jasonfurman), "Poorly designed, temporary, deficit-financed tax cuts have been consistently shown to reduce growth which will lower wages, not raise them," Twitter, October 16, 2017, 10:11 a.m., https://twitter.com/jasonfurman/status/919928885994811392.

19. MSNBC, "Sen. Schumer Talks Tax Plan with Rachel Maddow," Facebook, November 2, 2017, https://www.facebook.com/watch/?v=1798987900197454.

20. Martin Wolf, "A Republican Tax Plan Built for Plutocrats," *Financial Times*, November 21, 2017, https://www.ft.com/content/e494f47e-ce1a-11e7-9dbb-291a884dd8c6.

21. Cristina Marcos and Naomi Jagoda, "The 13 House Republicans Who Voted against the GOP Tax Plan," *The Hill*, November 16, 2017, https://thehill.com/homenews/house/360780-the-13-house-republicans-who-voted-against-the-gop-tax-plan.

22. George Will, "Planning for the Future Is Impossible. It's Also This Man's Job," *Washington Post*, October 20, 2017, https://www.washingtonpost.com/opinions/planning-for-the-future-is-impossible-its-also-this-mans-job/2017/10/20/6d1c4196-b500-11e7-be94-fabb0f1e9ffb_story.html.

23. Larry Kudlow, "Kevin Hassett Spanks the Tax Policy Center on Taxes and Growth," CNBC, October 7, 2017, https://www.cnbc.com/2017/10/07/kudlow-kevin-hassett-spanks-the-tax-policy-center.html.

24. Abha Bhattarai, "Walmart Said It's Giving Its Employees a Raise. And Then It Closed 63 Stores," *Washington Post*, January 11, 2018, https://www.washingt onpost.com/news/business/wp/2018/01/11/walmart-to-raise-starting-hourly-wa ge-to-11-offer-paid-parental-leave/.

25. Luke Stangel, "Apple Celebrates Trump's Tax Cut with $2,500 Bonuses for All Employees," *Silicon Valley Business Journal*, January 18, 2018, https://www.biz journals.com/sanjose/news/2018/01/18/apple-trump-tax-cut-employee-bonuses -aapl.html.

26. "JPMorgan Chase to Open 400 New Branches," Finextra, January 24, 2018, https://www.finextra.com/newsarticle/31568/jpmorgan-chase-to-open-400-new -branches.

27. Gary Cohn and Kevin Hassett, "Tax Reform Has Delivered for Workers," *Wall Street Journal*, October 12, 2021, https://www.wsj.com/articles/tax-reform-has -delivered-for-workers-11577045463.

28. Ibid.

29. "African-American Economic Impact," White House internal document.

30. Ibid.

31. "Trump Says 'Not Even a Little Bit Happy' with Feds Powell: Report," Reuters, November 27, 2018, https://www.reuters.com/article/us-usa-trump-fed/trump -says-not-even-a-little-bit-happy-with-feds-powell-report-idUSKCN1NW2LO.

32. Brian Cheung, "Trump Has Tweeted about the Fed 100 Times since Nominating Jerome Powell," Yahoo!, January 26, 2020, https://www.yahoo .com/now/trumps-twitter-criticism-of-the-federal-reserve-fades-after-rate-cuts -124538265.html.

33. Fred Imbert, "U.S. Stocks Post Worst Year in a Decade as the S&P 500 Falls More Than 6% in 2018," CNBC, December 31, 2018, https://www.cnbc.com /2018/12/31/stock-market-wall-street-stocks-eye-us-china-trade-talks.html; "Fed Chair's Job Is Not in Jeopardy, White House Economic Adviser Says," Reuters, December 26, 2018, https://www.reuters.com/article/uk-usa-trump-fed /fed-chairs-job-is-not-in-jeopardy-white-house-economic-adviser-says-idUKKC N1OP0ZZ.

## Chapter Seven
## Five Million Hours and Counting

1. Casey B. Mulligan, *You're Hired!: Untold Successes and Failures of a Populist President* (Washington, D.C.: Republic Book Publishers, 2020), 156.

2. Ibid., 164.

3. Ibid.

4. "The Jones Act, A Legacy of Economic Ruin for Puerto Rico," John Dunham and Associates, February 2019, http://www.camarapr.org/Ponencias-Kenneth /The-Jones-Act-A-Legacy-Economic-Ruins.pdf.

5. Ibid.

6. Mulligan, *You're Hired!* 164.

7.  David R. Henderson, "How the Jones Act Harms America," Hoover Institution, October 7, 2019, https://www.hoover.org/research/how-jones-act-harms-ame rica.
8.  "Exxon, Qatar to Start Construction on Texas Golden Pass LNG Export Plant," Reuters, May 9, 2019, https://www.reuters.com/article/us-exxon-lng-gol den-pass/exxon-qatar-to-start-construction-on-texas-golden-pass-lng-export-pl ant-idUSKCN1SF1UM.
9.  Mulligan, *You're Hired!* 158.
10. Ibid., 164.
11. Chang-Tai Hsieh and Enrico Moretti, "Housing Constraints and Spatial Misallocation," *American Economic Journal: Macroeconomics* 11, no. 2 (April 2019): 1–39, https://www.aeaweb.org/articles?id=10.1257/mac.20170388.
12. "Economic Report of the President," Council of Economic Advisers, February 2018, https://www.govinfo.gov/content/pkg/ERP-2018/pdf/ERP-2018.pdf.
13. Ibid.
14. "Regulatory Reform," U.S. Chamber of Commerce, https://www.uschamber .com/regulatory-reform.
15. Clyde Crews, "Trump Regulations: Federal Register Page Count Is Lowest in Quarter Century," Competitive Enterprise Institute, December 29, 2017, https:// cei.org/blog/trump-regulations-federal-register-page-count-is-lowest-in-quarter -century/.
16. Internal memo, Council of Economic Advisers.
17. Keith B. Belton and John D. Graham, "Deregulation under Trump," Regulation, Cato Institute, Summer 2020, https://www.cato.org/regulation/summer-2020/ deregulation-under-trump.
18. Clyde Crews and Kent Lassman, "New Ten Thousand Commandments Report Evaluates the Sweeping Hidden Tax of Regulation; Provides Definitive Assessment of Trump Deregulatory Legacy," Competitive Enterprise Institute, June 30, 2021, https://cei.org/studies/ten-thousand-commandments-2020/.
19. "Economic Report of the President," Council of Economic Advisers, (chart) 85.
20. "Economic Report of the President," Council of Economic Advisers, (chart) 96.
21. Donald Trump, "Executive Order 13777," Federal Register, National Archives, February 24, 2017, https://www.federalregister.gov/documents/2017/03/01/20 17-04107/enforcing-the-regulatory-reform-agenda.
22. "Economic Report of the President," Council of Economic Advisers, 95.
23. Timothy Doyle, "EPA's New Cost-Benefit Rule Is a Big Win for Everyone," Issues and Insights, July 28, 2020, https://issuesinsights.com/2020/07/28/epas -new-cost-benefit-rule-is-a-big-win-for-everyone/.
24. Ibid.
25. Susan E. Dudley, "Trump's Deregulatory Promises Are Coming True," *The Hill*, December 15, 2017, https://thehill.com/opinion/white-house/365130-trumps -deregulatory-promises-are-coming-true-and-saving-570-million.
26. Internal memo, Council of Economic Advisers.

27.  Pamela Glass, "Made in the USA: The Jones Act," Workboat, September 4, 2020, https://www.workboat.com/government/trump-biden-support-the-jones -act.

28.  "Biden's Worst Executive Order Went Almost Entirely Unnoticed," Issues and Insights, January 29, 2021, https://issuesinsights.com/2021/01/29/bidens-worst -executive-order-went-almost-entirely-unnoticed/.

29.  Ibid.

30.  Ibid.; Kevin Robillard, "The Game-Changing Biden Order You Haven't Heard About," HuffPost, January 24, 2021, https://www.huffpost.com/entry/biden-or der-progressive-regulation_n_6009dabec5b6efae63002e20.

31.  Ibid.

32.  "Biden's Worst Executive Order Went Almost Entirely Unnoticed," Issues and Insights.

## Chapter Eight
## What Makes a Country a Country

1.  Ronald Reagan, "Remarks at the Presentation Ceremony for the Presidential Medal of Freedom," Archives, Ronald Reagan Presidential Library and Museum, January 19, 1989, https://www.reaganlibrary.gov/archives/speech/ remarks-presentation-ceremony-presidential-medal-freedom-5.

2.  Donald Trump, "Remarks by President Trump on Modernizing Our Immigration System for a Stronger America," Remarks, Trump White House Archives, May 16, 2019, https://trumpwhitehouse.archives.gov/briefings-sta tements/remarks-president-trump-modernizing-immigration-system-stronger -america/.

3.  Trevor English, "What Percentage of Engineering Graduates Actually Work in Their Respective Fields," Interesting Engineering, March 14, 2021, https:// interestingengineering.com/what-percentage-of-engineering-graduates-actually -work-in-their-respective-fields.

4.  Trump, "Remarks by President Trump on Modernizing Our Immigration System for a Stronger America."

5.  Ibid.

6.  "Opinion: Trump's Immigration Plan Is an Improvement. It's Also an Act of Political Positioning," Washington Post, May 16, 2019, https://www.washington post.com/opinions/trumps-immigration-plan-is-an-improvement-its-also-an-act -of-political-positioning/2019/05/16/9f90dea8-77fe-11e9-b7ae-390de4259661 _story.html.

7.  Brett Samuels, "Kushner Says He'll Present Immigration Plan to Trump in Coming Days," The Hill, April 23, 2019, https://thehill.com/homenews/adminis tration/440211-kushner-says-hell-present-immigration-plan-to-trump-in-co ming-days.

## Chapter Nine
## The Fruits of Leverage Diplomacy

1. Benny Morris, "Camp David and After: An Exchange," *New York Review of Books*, June 13, 2002, https://www.nybooks.com/articles/2002/06/13/camp-da vid-and-after-an-exchange-1-an-interview-wi/.

2. "Israel's Diplomatic Giant Eban Dies," BBC News, November 18, 2002, http://news.bbc.co.uk/2/hi/middle_east/2486473.stm.

3. Donald Trump, "Peace to Prosperity: A Vision to Improve the Lives of the Palestinian and Israeli People," Trump White House Archives, June 21, 2019, https://trumpwhitehouse.archives.gov/peacetoprosperity/.

4. Hernando De Soto, "The Capitalist Cure for Terrorism," *Wall Street Journal*, October 10, 2014, https://www.wsj.com/articles/the-capitalist-cure-for-terrori sm-1412973796.

5. Ibid.

6. Ibid.

7. Ibid.

8. Jeffrey Sonnenfeld, "The Bahrain Conference: What the Experts and the Media Missed," *Fortune*, June 30, 2019, https://fortune.com/2019/06/30/bahrain-sum mit-middle-east/; Jared Kushner, "Press Release - Remarks by White House Senior Advisor Jared Kushner at the Peace to Prosperity Workshop," American Presidency Project, June 25, 2019, https://www.presidency.ucsb.edu/documents /press-release-remarks-white-house-senior-advisor-jared-kushner-the-peace-pros perity.

9. Raphael Ahren, "In Bahrain, Kushner Urges Absent Palestinians to Seize 'Opportunity of Century,'" *Times of Israel*, June 25, 2019, https://www.timeso fisrael.com/opening-bahrain-workshop-kushner-says-economic-progress-a-pre condition-to-peace/.

10. Ibid.

11. Bernard Avishai, "Why Jared Kushner's Bahrain Conference Won't Do Much for the Palestinian Economy," *New Yorker*, June 29, 2019, https://www.newyor ker.com/news/daily-comment/why-jared-kushners-bahrain-conference-wont-do -much-for-the-palestinian-economy.

12. Ahren, "In Bahrain, Kushner Urges Absent Palestinians to Seize 'Opportunity of Century.'"

13. Avishai, "Why Jared Kushner's Bahrain Conference Won't Do Much for the Palestinian Economy."

14. Sonnenfeld, "The Bahrain Conference: What the Experts and the Media Missed."

15. Ibid.

16. Quint Forgey, "'The Dawn of a New Middle East': Trump Celebrates Abraham Accords with White House Signing Ceremony," *Politico*, September 15, 2020, https://www.politico.com/news/2020/09/15/trump-abraham-accords-palestinia ns-peace-deal-415083.

17.  Jim Tankersley, "Where Spider-Man and Captain America Intern: The White House Economic Team," *New York Times*, March 19, 2019, https://www.nyt imes.com/2019/03/19/us/politics/interns-council-economic-advisers.html.

## Chapter Ten
## Socialism and Trump's Place in History

1.   Frank Newport, "The Meaning of 'Socialism' to Americans Today," Gallup, October 4, 2018, https://news.gallup.com/opinion/polling-matters/243362/mea ning-socialism-americans-today.aspx.
2.   "The Opportunity Costs of Socialism," Council of Economic Advisers, October 2018, https://trumpwhitehouse.archives.gov/wp-content/uploads/2018/10/The -Opportunity-Costs-of-Socialism.pdf.
3.   Tom Phillips, "Xi Jinping Thought to Be Taught in China's Universities," *The Guardian*, October 27, 2017, https://www.theguardian.com/world/2017/oct/27/ xi-jinping-thought-to-be-taught-in-chinas-universities.
4.   Maya Angelou (@DrMayaAngelou), "When someone shows you who they are, believe them the first time," Twitter, June 12, 2015, 12:01 p.m., https://twitter .com/drmayaangelou/status/609390085604311040?lang=en.
5.   James Gwartney, Robert Lawson, and Joshua Hall, *Economic Freedom of the World: 2016 Annual Report*, Fraser Institute, 2016, https://www.fraserinstitute .org/sites/default/files/economic-freedom-of-the-world-2016.pdf.
6.   "World Economic Freedom Index, 2018," Fraser Institute, https://www.fraserin stitute.org/economic-freedom/dataset?geozone=world&year=2018&p age=dataset&min-year=2&max-year=0&filter=0&page=datase t&min-year=2&max-year=0&filter=0.
7.   Jan-Werner Muller, *What Is Populism?* (Philadelphia: University of Pennsylvania Press, 2016), 13.
8.   World Bank, "Venezuelan Migration: The 4,500-Kilometer Gap between Desperation and Opportunity," November 26, 2019, https://www.worldbank .org/en/news/feature/2019/11/26/migracion-venezolana-4500-kilometros-entre -el-abandono-y-la-oportunidad.
9.   "The Opportunity Costs of Socialism," Council of Economic Advisers, October 2018, 2, https://trumpwhitehouse.archives.gov/wp-content/uploads/2018/10 /The-Opportunity-Costs-of-Socialism.pdf.
10.  Ibid.
11.  Matthew Yglesias, "Elizabeth Warren Has a Plan to Save Capitalism," Vox, August 15, 2018, https://www.vox.com/2018/8/15/17683022/elizabeth-warren -accountable-capitalism-corporations.
12.  Edward Lazear, "Socialism, Capitalism, and Income," Hoover Institution, May 12, 2020, https://www.hoover.org/research/socialism-capitalism-and-income.
13.  Ibid.
14.  "The Opportunity Costs of Socialism," 26.

15. Michael E. McKenney, "Inappropriate Criteria Were Used to Identify Tax-Exempt Applications for Review," May 14, 2013, https://www.treasury.gov/tig ta/auditreports/2013reports/201310053fr.pdf.

16. "Incomes Hit a Record High and Poverty Reached a Record Low in 2019," Council of Economic Advisers, September 15, 2020, https://trumpwhitehouse.ar chives.gov/articles/incomes-hit-record-high-poverty-reached-record-low-2019/ ?utm_source=facebook&utm_medium=social&utm_campaign=wh.

17. Joseph Schumpeter, *Capitalism, Socialism and Democracy* (United Kingdom: Routledge, 2010), 131.

18. Ibid, 136.

19. Ibid, 137.

20. Ibid.

21. Josh Hawley, "Senator Hawley Introduces the 'Trust-Busting for the Twenty-First Century Act': A Plan to Bust Up Anti-Competitive Big Businesses," April 12, 2021, https://www.hawley.senate.gov/senator-hawley-introduces-trust-bus ting-twenty-first-century-act-plan-bust-anti-competitive-big.

22. Ibid.

23. Schumpeter, 136.

24. "Bernie Sanders on the Issues," Issues, BernieSanders.com, https://berniesanders .com/issues/.

25. Jenni Fink, "Almost 80 Percent of Philosophy Majors Favor Socialism, Poll Finds," *Newsweek*, July 15, 2019, https://www.newsweek.com/socialism-philos ophy-majors-college-poll-1449238.

26. Jon Street, "Less than 2 Percent of Harvard Faculty Are Conservative, Survey Finds," *Campus Reform*, March 2020, https://www.campusreform.org/?ID=1 4469.

27. Karl Marx, *A Contribution to the Critique of Hegel's Philosophy of Right*, 1843, https://www.marxists.org/archive/marx/works/1843/critique-hpr/intro .htm.

28. Schumpeter, 127.

29. Ibid, 5.

30. Ibid.

31. "Social Issues Attract Executive Council's Attention," Episcopal News Service, October 27, 2014, https://www.episcopalnewsservice.org/2014/10/27/social-issu es-attract-executive-councils-attention/. This page has since been taken down; "EPPN: Urge Your Senator to Raise the Minimum Wage," Office of Government Relations, The Episcopal Church, April 8, 2014, https://www.epis copalchurch.org/ogr/eppn-urge-your-senator-to-raise-the-minimum-wage/.

32. Joshua Rhett Miller, "BLM Site Removes Page on 'Nuclear Family Structure' Amid NFL Vet's Criticism," *New York Post*, September 24, 2020, https://nypost .com/2020/09/24/blm-removes-website-language-blasting-nuclear-family-struc ture/#:~:text=Black%20Lives%20Matter%20scrubbed%20a,misinterpreting %20the%20organization's%20incendiary%20message.

33. Minnesota Psychological Association, *Father-Absent Homes: Implications for Criminal Justice and Mental Health Professionals*, August 4, 2021, https://www.mnpsych.org/index.php%3Foption%3Dcom_dailyplanetblog%26view%3Dentry%26category%3Dindustry%2520news%26id%3D54.

34. Elizabeth Wildsmith, Jennifer Manlove, and Elizabeth Cook, "Dramatic Increase in the Proportion of Births outside of Marriage in the United States from 1990 to 2016," ChildTrends, August 8, 2018, https://www.childtrends.org/publications/dramatic-increase-in-percentage-of-births-outside-marriage-among-whites-hispanics-and-women-with-higher-education-levels.

35. Schumpeter, 116.

36. Alma Cohen, Moshe Hazan, Roberto Tallarita, and David Weiss, *The Politics of CEOs*, National Bureau of Economic Research, May 2019, https://www.nber.org/papers/w25815.

37. Kevin Hassett and John Lott, "Is Newspaper Coverage of Economic Events Politically Biased?" *Public Choice* 160, no. 1/2 (2014): 65–108, https://www.jstor.org/stable/24507639.

38. Hans G. Hassell, John B. Holbein, and Matthew R. Miles, "There Is No Liberal Bias in Which Stories Political Journalists Decide to Cover," *Science Advances* 6, no. 14 (April 1, 2020), https://advances.sciencemag.org/content/6/14/eaay9344.

39. Hassett and Lott, "Is Newspaper Coverage of Economic Events Politically Biased?"

40. Schumpeter, 144.

# Chapter Eleven
## The Way Forward

1. William Manchester and Paul Reid, *The Last Lion: Winston Spencer Churchill, Defender of the Realm, 1940–1965* (New York: Little, Brown and Company, 2012), 941.

2. F. A. Hayek, *The Road to Serfdom: Texts and Documents: The Definitive Edition* (London: Routledge, 2008), 159.

3. Ibid.

4. Manchester and Reid, *The Last Lion*, 943.

5. Daniel Villarreal, "Kamala Harris More Liberal Than Bernie Sanders, Senate Record Analysis Shows," *Newsweek*, August 11, 2020, https://www.newsweek.com/kamala-harris-more-liberal-bernie-sanders-senate-record-analysis-shows-1524481.

6. Marshall McLuhan and Quentin Fiore, *The Medium Is the Message: An Inventory of Effects* (California: Gingko Press, 2001), 26.

7. Marshall McLuhan, "Interview on The Education of Mike McManus," TVOntario, December 1977, https://www.youtube.com/watch?v=_d5Tma2KKrc.

8. Marshall McLuhan, "Interview with Eric Norden," *Playboy*, March 1969; Marshall McLuhan and Bruce R. Powers, *The Global Village* (Oxford: Oxford University Press, 1992).

9.  Marshall McLuhan, *Understanding Media: The Extensions of Man* (1964; repr., Boston: MIT Press, 1994).

10. Marshall McLuhan, interview with Robert Fulford, Canadian Broadcasting Corporation TV, May 8, 1966.

11. McLuhan and Powers, *The Global Village*, 92.

12. Tamara Keith, "From 'Covfefe' to Slamming CNN: Trump's Year in Tweets," NPR, December 20, 2017, npr.org/2017/12/20/571617079/a-year-of-the-trump -presidency-in-tweets.

13. Barbara Bickart, Susan Fournier, and Martin Nisenholtz, "What Trump Understands about Using Social Media to Drive Attention," *Harvard Business Review*, March 1, 2017, https://hbr.org/2017/03/what-trump-understands-abo ut-using-social-media-to-drive-attention.

14. Ibid.

15. Justin Baragona, "Google Threatens to Ban Right-Wing Site The Federalist from Its Ad Platform," The Daily Beast, June 16, 2020, https://www.thedailybeast .com/google-bans-right-wing-site-the-federalist-from-its-ad-platform.

16. Will Feuer, "Conservative Group Slams Nike, Coke, and American Airlines over 'Woke Politics'," *New York Post*, May 19, 2021, https://nypost.com/2021/05/19/ conservative-group-slams-nike-coke-over-woke-politics/.

17. Ian Schwartz, "Trump: 'America Will Never Be a Socialist Country'; 'We Were Born Free and We Will Stay Free'," RealClearPolitics, February 5, 2019, https:// www.realclearpolitics.com/video/2019/02/05/trump_america_will_never_be _a_socialist_country_we_were_born_free_and_we_shall_stay_free.html.

# Index